University of Notre Dame
Notre Dame, Indiana

Written by Anikka M. Ayala
Edited by William Scheff, Mo Mozuch

Additional contributions by Omid Gohari,
Christina Koshzow, Chris Mason, Joey Rahimi,
Jon Skindzier, Luke Skurman, Tim Williams,
Kristine Rodriguez and James Balzer

ISBN # 1-59658-170-0
ISSN # 1552-1648
© Copyright 2005 College Prowler
All Rights Reserved
Printed in the U.S.A.
www.collegeprowler.com

Special thanks to Babs Carryer, Andy Hannah, LaunchCyte, Tim O'Brien, Bob Sehlinger, Thomas Emerson, Andrew Skurman, Barbara Skurman, Bert Mann, Dave Lehman, Daniel Fayock, Chris Babyak,The Donald H. Jones Center for Entrepreneurship, Terry Slease, Jerry McGinnis, Bill Ecenberger, Idie McGinty, Kyle Russell, Jacque Zaremba, Larry Winderbaum, Paul Kelly, Roland Allen, Jon Reider, Team Evankovich, Julie Fenstermaker, Lauren Varacalli, Abu Noaman, Jason Putorti, Mark Exler, Daniel Steinmeyer, Jared Cohon, Gabriela Oates, Tri Ad Litho, David Koegler, and Glen Meakem.

Bounce Back Team: Kate Lindsey, Caitlin Kennelly, Kate Burmon, Laura Froyen, and Chuy Benitez

College Prowler™
5001 Baum Blvd.
Suite 456
Pittsburgh, PA 15213

Phone: (412) 697-1390, 1(800) 290-2682
Fax: (412) 697-1396, 1(800) 772-4972
E-mail: info@collegeprowler.com
Website: www.collegeprowler.com

Welcome to College Prowler™

During the writing of College Prowler's guidebooks, we felt it was critical that our content was unbiased and unaffiliated with any college or university. We think it's important that our readers get honest information and a realistic impression of the student opinions on any campus — that's why if any aspect of a particular school is terrible, we (unlike a campus brochure) intend to publish it. While we do keep an eye out for the occasional extremist — the cheerleader or the cynic — we take pride in letting the students tell it like it is. We strive to create a book that's as representative as possible of each particular campus. Our books cover both the good and the bad, and whether the survey responses point to recurring trends or a variation in opinion, these sentiments are directly and proportionally expressed through our guides.

College Prowler guidebooks are in the hands of students throughout the entire process of their creation. Because you can't make student-written guides without the students, we have students at each campus who help write, randomly survey their peers, edit, layout, and perform accuracy checks on every book that we publish. From the very beginning, student writers gather the most up-to-date stats, facts, and inside information on their colleges. They fill each section with student quotes and summarize the findings in editorial reviews. In addition, each school receives a collection of letter grades (A through F) that reflect student opinion and help to represent contentment, prominence, or satisfaction for each of our 20 specific categories. Just as in grade school, the higher the mark the more content, more prominent, or more satisfied the students are with the particular category.

Once a book is written, additional students serve as editors and check for accuracy even more extensively. Our bounce-back team — a group of randomly selected students who have no involvement with the project — are asked to read over the material in order to help ensure that the book accurately expresses every aspect of the university and its students. This same process is applied to the 200-plus schools College Prowler currently covers. Each book is the result of endless student contributions, hundreds of pages of research and writing, and countless hours of hard work. All of this has led to the creation of a student information network that stretches across the nation to every school that we cover. It's no easy accomplishment, but it's the reason that our guides are such a great resource.

When reading our books and looking at our grades, keep in mind that every college is different and that the students who make up each school are not uniform — as a result, it is im-portant to assess schools on a case-by-case basis. Because it's impossible to summarize an entire school with a single number or description, each book provides a dialogue, not a decision, that's made up of 20 different topics and hundreds of student quotes. In the end, we hope that this guide will serve as a valuable tool in your college selection process. Enjoy!

OMID GOHARI ◯ CHRISTINA KOSHZOW ◯ CHRIS MASON ◯ JOEY RAHIMI ◯ LUKE SKURMAN ◯
The College Prowler™ Team

Table of Contents

Introduction from the Author

When I was a little girl, every time someone asked me where I wanted to go to school when I was older, I'd stand up proud and tall, stick out my chest authoritatively and announce, "I want to go to Notre Dame." I didn't say that because I'm a legacy, or because I had seen the movie "Rudy" (which I didn't see until I was a Freshmen at ND). I'm not really sure when or how I first heard the words "Notre Dame," but they always sat quietly in the recesses of my mind.

The first time I visited Notre Dame, I knew why I wanted to go to school there. Driving up Notre Dame Avenue, I saw the Golden Dome, shimmering in the afternoon light; I saw the Basilica's bell tower, colored with history, standing erect and overlooking the campus with a caring eye. During that weekend visit I witnessed, first-hand, the academic excellence and family atmosphere that are a part of the Notre Dame tradition.

Established in 1842 by French monk Father Edward Sorin, Notre Dame was founded on the principles of Catholic faith and perseverance. Through the years, Notre Dame has carved a reputation of academic excellence. With 763 full-time faculty members, a student/teacher ratio of 12:1, seven schools, including a Graduate Program and Law School, and approximately thirty-eight majors, Notre Dame is slowly building a liberal arts tradition rivaling that of some Ivy League universities. Boasting a combined total of twenty-four varsity teams, forty-eight club and intramural sports teams, and over 300 student organizations, Notre Dame strives to mold excellence outside the classroom as well.

If you are already considering Notre Dame as one of your college choices, you've probably heard all of this before, and right now, you're probably wondering whether or not it's all true. Well, here's your chance to find out the truth, straight from the mouths of the students. Welcome to the College Prowler Guidebook on the University of Notre Dame. I sincerely hope that this book sheds light on the reasons why I and so many other students chose to go to Notre Dame, and I hope it aids you in your search for the college that's right for you.

Anikka M. Ayala, Author
University of Notre Dame

By the Numbers

General Information

University of Notre Dame
Notre Dame, Indiana 46556

Control:
Private

Academic Calendar:
Semester

Religious Affiliation:
Catholic

Founded:
1842

Website:
www.nd.edu

Main Phone:
(574) 631-5000

Admissions Phone:
(574) 631-7505

Student Body

**Full-Time
Undergraduates:**
8293

**Full-Time Male
Undergraduates:**
4441 (53%)

**Full-Time Female
Undergraduates:**
3970 (47%)

Admissions

Overall Acceptance Rate:
29%

Total Applicants:
12,095

Total Acceptances:
3,524

Freshman Enrollment:
1,996

Yield (% of Admitted Students who Actually Enroll):
57%

Applicants Placed on Waiting List:
840

Applicants Accepted From Waiting List:
572

Students Enrolled From Waiting List:
142

Transfer Applications Received:
549

Transfer Applications Accepted:
199

Transfer Students Enrolled:
165

Transfer Student Yield:
83%

Early Decision Available?
No

Early Action Available?
Yes

Early Action Acceptance Rate:
50%

Early Action Deadline:
November 1

Early Action Notification:
Dec. 25

Regular Decision Deadline:
Jan. 9

Regular Decision Notification:
Apr. 5

Must-Reply-By Date:
May 1

Common Application Accepted?
No

Supplemental Forms?
No

Admissions Phone:
(574) 631-7505

Admissions E-mail:
admissio.1@nd.edu

Admissions Website:
http://admissions.nd.edu/

SAT I or ACT Required?
Either

**SAT I Range
(25th – 75th Percentile):**
1270-1460

**SAT I Verbal Range
(25th – 75th Percentile):**
620-720

**SAT I Math Range
(25th – 75th Percentile):**
650-740

ACT Composite:
30-33

Top 10% of High Scool Class:
83%

Application Fee:
$50

Financial Information

Full-Time Tuition:
$29,512

Room and Board:
$7,418

Books and Supplies for class:
$850

**Average Need-Based
Financial Aid Package:**
$23,412

**Students Who
Applied For Financial Aid:**
56%

Students Who Received Aid:
48%

Financial Aid Forms Deadline:
February 15th

Financial Aid Phone:
(574) 631-6436

Financial Aid Website:
http://financialaid.nd.edu

Academics

The Lowdown On...
Academics

Degrees Awarded:
Bachelor
Master
Doctorate

Undergraduate Schools:
College of Arts and Letters
Mendoza College of Business
College of Engineering
School of Architecture

Most Popular Areas of Study:
Business (30%)
Engineering (10%)
Political Science (9%)
Pre-Medical (6%)
Psychology (6%)

→

**Four Year
Graduation Rate:**
88%

**Five Year
Graduation Rate:**
94%

**Six Year
Graduation Rate:**
95%

Full-Time Faculty:
763

**Faculty with
Terminal Degree:**
98%

**Student-to-Faculty
Ratio:**
12:1

Average Course Load:
15 hours

AP Test Score Requirements
Possible credit for scores of 4 or higher in select courses.

Sources for Academic Support
• First Year of Studies Free Tutoring

• NCAA tutors for athletes

• Free Review Sessions before departmental exams

• Free Wednesday night tutoring for select classes

• The University Writing Center

• Professors

• TAs

Did You Know?

The construction of an archive of student papers in Hesburg Library is currently being discussed by the ND Administration. This archive would be filled with papers that professors feel are exceptional; these papers would be available as examples to other students.

Best Places to Study
- Hesburg Library
- Coleman-Morse Study Lounge
- O'Shaughnessy Main Table
- La Fortune Student Center

Students Speak Out On...
Academics

"Classes are interesting depending on the teacher. Most teachers are fun and eager to teach, but others know their material too well and have a hard time teaching it to students."

Q "I really like all the teachers I've had. They are very personable, and you can talk to them. They're also very accessible, which is a good thing, if you have last minute questions or problems. For the most part, the **professors love what they're doing** and they make the classes interesting."

Q "I have had great experiences with my professors and I have had some fabulous TAs as well. It seems to me that **all the professors are very concerned about helping and teaching their students**. All the professors have been approachable, provide office hours, welcome emails, etc."

Q "Teachers are great. The professors are normally reachable and if you have the opportunity to take a class taught by a graduate student, take it. **TAs are usually nice and teach better than the full-fledged professors**."

Q "Most of my teachers have been great, and I think that they are representative of the faculty in general. **In my experience they are very open and care about student learning**. They will make time outside of their own normal office hours to meet with you and help you as long as you're willing to ask."

Q "Most of the teachers are great and are **very willing to give one-on-one assistance**. There is, of course, the occasional jerk who thinks he doesn't have time, but that's rare."

Q "The professors in the smaller courses take the time to get to know their students and really cater to teaching undergraduate students. They are very approachable and will do their best to help you when you need it. As far as the larger courses, the **TAs take the initiative to help students**. The professors for the large courses will help students, but they are not as approachable as the TAs."

Q "I love my teachers. Not only do **they really know what they are doing**, if I have any problems, they are also always available during office hours to answer any questions. Many of my teachers have invited classes to their houses for holidays and for dinner during the semester."

Q "One of the great things about Notre Dame is that your **classes are actually taught by professors**. Classes are interesting if you enjoy the subject matter. If you register for classes addressing subjects you truly want to learn more about then you'll find what you are looking for. "

Q "Just like any school, you'll run into some terrible foreign professors that don't care about you, but most of the classes aren't like that. My worst teacher couldn't teach Calculus even though she could probably use it to build a bomb. On the other hand, I had a professor that bought pizza for 300 kids after every exam, and he was a really good professor. Bottom line: **everything gets better as you slowly make your way into your major** and start taking smaller classes."

Q "Overall, the professors are friendly and willing to take extra time to help out students. My experience has shown me that **the professors here are very approachable** and interested in each student's learning."

Q "It's just like anywhere else–there are going to be great professors, and there are going to be some who aren't so hot. The thing is, here, **the good ones really outnumber the bad**."

The College Prowler Take On...
Academics

If you ever happen to watch a Notre Dame football game, you'll find the same advertisements being flashed between quarters: a snowy-bearded professor with a hearty laugh and rosy cheeks gently gives his students a pat on the back; a balding little man happily prances around before wide-eyed eager young minds as he teaches bio-chemistry. Well, this just might be one of those rare instances where advertisers aren't lying to you. Although some students occasionally encounter that one, bloodthirsty, 'Attila-the-Hun' professor who slashes at them with a red pen, this is relatively rare. Most students have found their professors to be enthusiastic, accessible and approachable. Even though they have all had some boring classes, the majority agrees that the classes required for their majors are more enjoyable and easy to praise.

The positive student quotes lead to high marks for Notre Dame academics. While there may be some professors who speak different languages or can't relate to their students, and there may be classes so boring that everyone's eyelids lose the battle with gravity, students are impressed with most of their classes. Notre Dame promises many academic hurdles, but the various sources of academic support—ranging from professors to TAs to university-sponsored tutoring programs—provide many hands to help students get through each semester.

The College Prowler™ Grade on
Academics: B+

A high Academics grade generally indicates that professors are knowledgeable, accessible, and genuinely interested in their students' welfare. Other determining factors include class size, how well professors communicate, and whether or not classes are engaging.

Local Atmosphere

The Lowdown On...
Local Atmosphere

Region:
Midwest

City, State:
Notre Dame, Indiana

Setting:
Small City

Distance from Indianapolis:
3 hours

Distance from Chicago:
2 hours

Points of Interest:
South Bend
Symphony Orchestra
College Football Hall of Fame
Potawatomi Zoo
Civic Center

Closest Shopping Malls:
College Park Mall

Closest Movie Theatres:

Cinemark 14
910 Edison Road
254-9685

Major Sports Teams:

Silverhawks (Minor League Baseball)

Local Events

- Potato Creek State Park, which offers picnicking, fishing and boating.
- The East Waterway brings mild white water rapids into South Bend.
- The Firefly Festival of the Performing Arts, an event which takes place each summer.

City Websites

http://aolsvc.digitalcity/southbend/

Students Speak Out On...
Local Atmosphere

{ **"The town isn't very big and often does not have the same 'college town' atmosphere that a state school might have, but you can see the school spirit in the entire community."**

Q "**South Bend is not a college town**. It is fairly dirty and not nice, but it won't really affect your day-to-day life. You might have a problem with theft if you move off-campus. There are two other universities nearby, but interaction with them is very limited."

Q "South Bend is not as bad as some people make it out to be. **There's plenty to do here**. The local civic center brings in many popular music groups, which are always fun to see."

Q "South Bend is not a university town—**Notre Dame is in a bubble**. South Bend is a very poor, industrial town with a lot of problems. The university is physically separated from the city."

Q "A lot of students find the neighborhood a bit rough–**it's not beautiful suburbia**. It would be nice to be closer to Chicago and in warmer weather, but there are many opportunities for service in the community."

Q "**The university is the biggest thing in town**. Everything is basically on-campus, but there are some cool spots downtown."

Q "South Bend, Indiana is not a great place. **The school is the best, but its location kind of sucks**. Although some may complain, it doesn't bother me. There's plenty to see on-campus, and Chicago is only an hour and a half away."

Q "You want to stay close to campus, as **South Bend is not the greatest city**, but you are within two hours of Chicago and Indianapolis."

Q "Coming from a larger city with almost a million people in the entire area, South Bend was a noticeable step down from the city atmosphere I was used to. I'm also from the Southwest, where mountains and rolling hills are abundant, so the flatness of the area and the horribly underdeveloped, ill-planned roads of South Bend would often leave me lost when I ventured off-campus. Most of the people in South Bend are very nice. **As nice as people are, though, it is not a good idea to go walking around South Bend at night**, especially to off-campus parties."

Q "South Bend is separated from ND. **I don't really feel like I live in a town**; I just feel like I live at Notre Dame."

The College Prowler Take On...
Local Atmosphere

At Notre Dame, a trip off-campus is not a fun-filled vacation in Beverly Hills (or a walk in the park, for that matter). As you can see, most students find the South Bend atmosphere to be disconcerting. The consensus is that this is not a quaint college town, but a dirty and somewhat dangerous small industrial city. While some students confess a longing for the relief of big city activities and attractions, most will admit that, although South Bend is not their favorite town, they find comfort in the isolation of the Notre Dame 'bubble.'

Notre Dame is so isolated from South Bend that it even has its own ZIP code. In the minds of many students, this is a good thing. South Bend is a poor city, and has many rough neighborhoods. While this may make it difficult for many students to feel comfortable venturing off-campus, leaving the Notre Dame 'bubble' to run an errand is a feasible idea, as long as you know what areas to avoid. However, the lack of student attractions and the disparaging comments from students leaves Notre Dame's location with low marks.

D-

The College Prowler™ Grade on
Local Atmosphere: D-

A high Local Atmosphere grade indicates that the area surrounding campus is safe and scenic. Other factors include nearby attractions, proximity to other schools, and the town's attitude toward students

Safety & Security

The Lowdown On...
Safety & Security

# of ND Police:
20

**Notre Dame
Police Phone:**
(574) 631-5555

Safety Services:
SafeWalk
Campus Shuttle

Health Services

The University of Notre Dame Health Services building is located on the North side of the university's campus, behind the Main Building. The Health Services Center is staffed by physicians Monday thru Friday from 9AM-4:30PM; Registered Nurses are available after these hours. The Health Center accepts walk-ins, and is equipped with a fourteen-bed inpatient unit that is willing and able to provide care to students recovering from surgical procedures, in need of intravenous fluids, medications, etc. In addition, the Health Center is also equipped with a lab and x-ray facilities, and is able to provide students with allergy injections, immunizations, and travel consultations.

For more information concerning the University of Notre Dame's Health Services Center, visit:

www.nd.edu/~uhs/ or call (574) 631-7479.

Students Speak Out On...
Safety & Security

"Security and safety are barely an issue. The campus itself is very safe, and the surrounding South Bend area is fairly safe as long as you know where you're going and don't get mixed up in bad neighborhoods."

Q "**I feel so safe on-campus**. Honestly, I'll walk around alone at night and it's not a big deal. There are emergency telephones around the lakes, which is nice. I know there is also a group that walks students to places, if you decide that you don't feel safe enough to walk yourself, but I've never used them."

Q "There is **generally a low crime level**. I can honestly say that I think I only locked the door to my room when I was leaving campus overnight and my roommate was not going to be there."

Q "I feel absolutely and completely safe on-campus at all times. The **campus itself is pretty enclosed; students often refer to it as the 'Notre Dame Bubble'**. The two lakes at the edge of campus are absolutely beautiful and walking around these at night might be a little sketchy, but there are 'blue lights' situated all around the lake and at the edges of campus. These lights have phones attached to them, allowing you to call for help if necessary."

Q "Notre Dame is very safe. There are the occasional bicycle thefts, but **I have never locked the door to my dorm room and most students never do either**. The campus is well lit, so getting around at night isn't a problem."

Q "Safety couldn't be better. **The school offers much in regard to student safety**. In fact, I've been told by just about everyone I know here that they honestly have no worries at all about on-campus safety. My sister walks around the lakes at one in the morning with no problems at all."

Q "The campus is pretty safe. I leave my door unlocked all the time and **I never feel threatened walking around at night**. They have a program called SafeWalk–if you're out there somewhere and don't want to walk by yourself, just give them a call and they come and walk with you. It's free."

Q "I feel very safe on-campus. While I would not go running by myself late at night, I don't feel uncomfortable walking across campus by myself in the evenings. We have a SafeWalk program where someone will walk with you if you want them to accompany you to your destination. Our campus is compact enough that **you really don't have to go far to get anywhere though**, so I don't feel the need to use the buddy system."

Q "The ND Security is actually really great at keeping Notre Dame a quiet and safe campus. **They patrol campus by car, bike, and ATV**, and are quick to respond to any reported trouble. If you are worried about walking at night from one end of campus to the other, they will gladly give you a ride. They will also give you a ride from your dorm to the bus stop and vice versa, if you live at the opposite end of campus or if the weather is really cold."

Q "As for as safety, I would have to say I felt safer at ND than I have ever felt in my hometown of El Paso. Maybe it's because at ND we were in our own little bubble and things like safety were taken for granted. **I never once had a second thought about walking alone at night** on-campus. I'm glad I didn't have to think about that."

The College Prowler Take On...
Safety & Security

These days, the thought of living in a safe neighborhood where no one locks their doors is just a memory of a time that existed on black and white television sets. Well, it seems that Notre Dame belongs back in the good old days. Aside from the occasional sneaky drunkard clumsily stealing a bike in the middle of the night, the majority of students agree: there is virtually no crime under the Golden Dome. Except on football weekends, many Notre Dame students say that they leave their dorm rooms unlocked. And, thanks to the small size of the campus, the presence of Notre Dame security, the blue light phones, and student organizations such as ND SafeWalk, most students confess to strolling along campus at all hours of the night without a care in the world.

The city of South Bend, however, is a stark contrast to campus. Students recommend avoiding many areas of the small industrial city, and some describe incidents where other students have had problems with theft and muggings while in South Bend. But most agree that these types of things can be avoided by skirting particular neighborhoods. While the Notre Dame campus is virtually crime-free, the atmosphere of the surrounding South Bend area brings down an otherwise top grade.

The College Prowler™ Grade on

Safety & Security: B+

A high grade in Safety & Security means that students generally feel safe, campus police are visible, blue-light phones and escort services are readily available, and safety precautions are not overly necessary.

Computers

The Lowdown On...
Computers

High-Speed Network?
Yes

Wireless Network?
Available in select locations

Number of Labs:
9

Number of Computers:
380

Cost to Print?
10 cents per page

24-Hour Labs:
- Fitzpatrick Hall rooms 148, 150, 170, 177
- LaFortune Student Center room 16
- Nieuwland Science Hall rooms 132, 202

Students Speak Out On...
Computers

"You should definitely bring a computer; you're going to have days when you want to work alone. On the other hand, the labs usually aren't crowded until finals near. And the network at Notre Dame is top notch."

"**Notre Dame has a ridiculous number of computers available throughout the campus**. You'll never have any problems once you find out where all the labs are, but having your own is nice."

"The computer situation on campus is not bad. There are many different computer clusters and at least one is open twenty-four hours. **Most people bring their own computers, but it is not necessary**. All dorm rooms are wired with Ethernet access."

"Bringing your own computer is by no means necessary. But I would recommend it. Being able to check your e-mail anytime is nice. Sometimes you may have to do quizzes online and may not feel like walking to one of the clusters in the cold or rain to get it done. I think **a laptop is even better—it's nice to be able to get out of your room** and go out on-campus to get your work done. One is especially useful when working on group projects."

"I would suggest bringing your own computer but if you don't have one or can't afford it, it's pretty easy to get access to one. I'm pretty sure that **every dorm has its own lab** with one or two computers, and there are other, much bigger labs all over campus."

Q "The network is nice but it comes across problems from time to time. **Stay away from clusters during midterms and finals**. Otherwise you'll probably always find a free one somewhere."

Q "The computer labs at ND are okay except during midterms or finals week. I worked at a lab for a year and I hated those weeks. The printers would jam and there would be lines forever and a day long. **If you have a computer and a printer: bring them**."

Q "Definitely bring your own computer. Computer labs are usually crowded, but definitely handy. **The network is usually decent**—I know nothing about technology, but I think it's okay."

Q "**It's a good idea to have your own computer**, but you can survive without one. Keep in mind that computer labs get crowded when big projects are due. If you don't have your own computer, make sure you don't procrastinate until the last second or you'll be fighting for a space in the lab."

Q "Having your own computer is convenient, especially when it's cold outside and during exams. The labs can get crowded during midterms and finals, but other than that, **you can get a computer whenever you need one**."

The College Prowler Take On...
Computers

A few words of wisdom to all you procrastinators: if you have a project due during finals week that requires completion in a computer cluster, make sure you have a gallon of coffee in hand, because you'll need it just to stay awake while you stand in line. Although Notre Dame provides nine computer clusters, four of which are open twenty-four hours a day, students agree that trying to gain access to a computer during midterms and finals week is a very difficult task. During the rest of the school year, however, most of the students say the network is fantastic. Probably the favorite aspect of the network is the speedy internet service in both clusters and dorm rooms. While everyone says that it's not impossible to survive without your own computer, having your own comes highly recommended. After all, it's so much more fun to instant-message friends from the comfort of your dorm room than a computer lab.

Although there is no way to argue against the freedom, convenience, and comfort of privacy that comes with having your own computer, the number of computer clusters, the existence of clusters in dorms, and the availability of Internet access in dorm rooms makes Notre Dame's computer network highly efficient. Just remember that you'll have a hard time breezing in and out of a computer lab during mid-terms or finals.

B

The College Prowler™ Grade on

Computers: B

A high grade in Computers designates that computer labs are available, the computer network is easily accessible, and the campus' computing technology is up-to-date.

Facilities

The Lowdown On...
Facilities

Campus Size:
1250 acres

Student Center:
La Fortune Student Center

Athletic Center:
Joyce Center
Rolf's Sport Recreation Cente
Knute Rockne Memorial
Building

Libraries:
10

Popular Places to Chill:
La Fortune Student Center
Recker's
Waddick's
Outside on the Quads during
warm weather.
2nd floor of the Hesburg
Library (for social studying)

Movie Theatre on Campus?

There is an unofficial movie theatre oncampus. The Student Union Board offers weekend movies in 101 and 102 DeBartolo Hall, the two largest classrooms on campus.

Bar on Campus?

Formally known as the Alumni Senior CLub, Legends of Notre Dame is a university run restaurant, bar, and night club that offers $2 maragritas on Thursdays (Senior Night) and dancing til 4 am on weekends.

On- campus Restaurants/Cafes

14

Bowling on Campus?

No.

What Is There to Do?

- Work out
- Watch a SUB-sponsored movie
- Go to Acoustic Café on Thursday nights
- Hang out in the student center
- Hang out at a campus restaurant/café
- Attend a multi-cultural event
- Attend an event sponsored by a dorm
- Check out a dance

Students Speak Out On...
Facilities

> "The facilities on campus are pretty good. They do a good job of maintaining the athletic facilities and even have extended hours to accommodate students."

Q "Everything is pretty good. There are three fitness facilities, and they're all modern and easy to use. The student center has a lot of cool stuff, too. **Basically, if you didn't want to leave campus, you wouldn't need to**, because everything's here—even a salon."

Q "The student center is nice, but nothing too wonderful. **We do have some really nice athletic facilities open to all students**."

Q "**Social space is kind of lacking**, but other than that everything is state-of-the-art. They're always building something new."

Q "**The student center is small compared to large public universities**, but it does have a Burger King and a Starbucks. There's also a mini grocery store similar to what you'd find at a gas station."

Q "You pay a lot to attend Notre Dame, and the facilities show it. **They're beautiful**."

Q "Notre Dame did not spare any expense while building any of its wonderful facilities. **They all meet the technologically advanced needs of professors and students today**, and almost all of the University's buildings, old and new, are architecturally beautiful to look at."

Q "The cafeterias are both nice, as are the athletic facilities. **Classrooms are comfortable**, although at times rather chilly! The student center (La Fortune) has recently undergone many renovations to add several amenities to the building (Starbucks, Subway, Sbarro) and has several other ideas brewing. Obviously, nothing is perfect, and there are always improvements to make, but overall, nothing is lacking."

Q "Rolfs and the Rock are great athletic facilities for anybody. I am not an athletic person and I was always able to find something I enjoyed doing. The student centers like La Fortune are nice, **but the dorms are the real student centers**."

Q "I love La Fortune! Subway and Starbucks...**what else could anybody possibly ask for?!**"

Q "**The facilities are great**. They're better than at most universities, especially in the athletic arena."

The College Prowler Take On...
Facilities

When you and your desk, bed, drawers, clothes, and miscellaneous furniture are forced to share a 14 x 14 space with another person, you're bound to get cabin fever unless you eventually leave your room. Thankfully, students feel that Notre Dame offers a number of high-quality student facilities which are as nice to look at as they are to frequent. With three different locations and an appeal to both serious and casual exercisers, the athletic facilities are ranked first in popularity among the students. Despite some complaints about a lack of variety and social space, the La Fortune Student Center comes in second with its collection of restaurants and a mini-convenience store.

Student praise for the athletic facilities and on-campus restaurants and cafes and the second floor study area of the Hesburg Library helps to offset the complaints about the minimal space at the student center. Overall, the variety, number, and condition of Notre Dame's facilities earn excellent marks.

The College Prowler™ Grade on

Facilities: A-

A high Facilities grade indicates that the campus is aesthetically pleasing and well-maintained; facilities are state-of-the-art, and libraries are exceptional. Other determining factors include the quality of both athletic and student centers and an abundance of things to do on campus.

Campus Dining

The Lowdown On...
Campus Dining

Freshman Meal Plan Requirement?
Yes

Meal Plan Average Cost:
$1870

Type of Meal Plans:
- Flex 14 (14 meals per week plus "Flex Points" for campus restaurants)
- Premium 21 (21 meals per week plus "Domer Dollars" to use in campus restaurants and at the Bookstore)

Places to Grab a Bite with Your Meal Plan

Burger King
Location: 1st Floor La Fortune Student Center

Food: Fast Food

Hours: Monday-Friday 8:30 a.m.-8 p.m.; Saturday 11 a.m.-8 p.m.; Sunday 11 a.m.-12 a.m.

Café de Gratsa
Location: 1st Floor Grace Hall

Food: Pastries, Pasta Stir-fry, Sandwiches, Fountain and Bottled Drinks

Hours: Monday-Friday 7 a.m.-3 p.m.

→

Café Ponche

Location: Bond Hall

Food: Deli Sandwiches, Baked Potatoes, Soda Bread, Cappuccinos and Fountain Drinks

Hours: Monday-Friday
7 a.m.-5 p.m.

Common Stock Sandwich Co.

Location: Mendoza College of Business

Food: Hot dogs, Yogurt, Fountain Drinks

Hours: Monday-Friday
7:30 a.m.-3:30 p.m.

Decio Commons

Location: 1st Floor Decio Faculty Hall

Food: Hot Soups, Fountain Drinks, Coffee

Hours: Monday-Friday 7 a.m.-3 p.m.

Greenfield's International Café

Location: 1st Floor Hesburg Center for International Studies

Food: Mushroom Soffrito, Black Bean Enchiladas, Chicken Pasta Alfredo

Hours: Monday-Friday
7 a.m.-2:30 p.m.

Irish Café

Location: Lower Level of Vicky Moore Law School

Food: Baked Goods, Cold Entrees, Fountain Drinks

Hours: Monday-Friday
7 a.m.-7 p.m.

Legends of Notre Dame

Location: East of Debartolo Center for the Performing Arts

Hours:
Luncheon: Monday-Friday
11:30 a.m.-2 p.m.

Dinner: Monday-Friday
4 p.m.-9 p.m.

Pub Hours: Monday-Wednesday 4 p.m.-12 a.m.

Thursday-Saturday 4 p.m.-2 a.m. Closed Sundays

The Morris Inn

Location: East of Welsh Family Hall

Hours: Breakfast:
7 a.m.-10:30 a.m.

Luncheon: 11:30 a.m.-2 p.m.

Dinner: 5:30 p.m.-8:30 p.m.

On Sundays, meals are available from 8 a.m.-3 p.m. and 4:30 p.m.-8:30 p.m.

Recker's

Location: South End of South Dining Hall

Food: Pizza, Burgers, Sandwiches, Fountain Drinks, Coffee, Smoothies, and Breakfast Foods

Hours: Open 24 Hours

Sbarro

Location: Basement of La Fortune Student Center

Food: Pizza, Pasta, Stromboli, Buffalo Wings

Hours: Monday-Wednesday 11 a.m.-2 a.m.; Thursday-Friday 11 a.m.-4 a.m.; Saturday 6 p.m.-4 a.m.; Sunday 6 p.m.-2 a.m.

Starbucks

Location: 1st Floor La Fortune Student Center

Food: Coffee and Pastries

Hours: Monday-Wednesday 7:30 a.m.-2 a.m.

Thursday-Friday 9:30 a.m.-4 a.m.; Saturday 9:30 a.m.-4 a.m.; Sunday 9:30 a.m.-2 a.m.

Subway

Location: 1st Floor La Fortune Student Center

Food: Soups, Salads, and Sandwiches

Hours: Monday-Friday 9:30 a.m.-1 a.m.; Saturday-Sunday 11 a.m.-1 a.m.

Waddick's

Location: 1st Floor O'Shaughnessy Hall

Food: Specialty Coffees, Soups

Hours: Monday-Friday 7 a.m.-5 p.m.

Warren Grille

Location: Warren Golf Course

Food: Focaccia Sandwiches, Gourmet Burgers, Muffins, Snacks

Hours: Sunday-Saturday 7 a.m.-7 p.m.; Closed 'til noon on Mondays

Off-Campus Places to Use Your Meal Plan:

None

24-Hour On-Campus Eating?

Recker's

Student Favorites:

Recker's
Burger King
Sbarro
Subway
Starbucks

Students Speak Out On...
Campus Dining

{ **"I think the dining hall food is a lot better than other schools. I got lucky; my dorm is right by South Dining Hall, which is a lot better than North, in my opinion."**

Q "You will live on-campus for at least three years and eat in the dining halls. **South Dining Hall is much better than North**, and as far as campus dining halls go they are the best in the country. You'll get tired of the food, but it will be like that anywhere."

Q "**Our food here is ranked second in the nation!** It's great for me, since I'm a varsity athlete and have an infinite number of meal points."

Q "**You will get tired of the food and crave mom's home cooking**, but it's really pretty good."

Q "The food on-campus is not bad at all; it's much better than many other schools I've visited. The dining halls offer a wide variety of foods. In each dining hall, there is a Mexican section, a cook-out section, a vegetarian section, a deli, a stir-fry section, a home cooking section and a Panini section. There's also a salad bar with fresh bread and soups! This may sound a little crazy, but **some parents want to eat in the dining hall when they visit** instead of going out to a restaurant."

Q "The dining hall is pretty good. We all complain, but **it's got a lot of options and there's usually something good to eat**. If you're really picky, it can be tough, but they do a good job."

Q "The dining halls at Notre Dame are number two in the nation, if that says anything. While the food is good, after several semesters on-campus, eating the same types of things every day does get old—there's never a time when I don't miss my mom's great cooking! That said, **the food is good and there are restaurants all over campus**."

Q "South dining hall is much better than North. It would be wise to learn the habits of the dining hall so you can **plan to eat during times when the food is the freshest**. You do have the option of getting a 'Grab-N-Go' sack lunch if you don't have time to stop and eat breakfast, lunch or dinner."

Q "You either like it or you hate it, but **it never beats mom's cooking**."

Q "Basically the dining halls are pretty good, **offering wide varieties of food** from Italian to Chinese, Mexican, grilled food, salad bar, desserts, breads etc. South Dining Hall is ranked number two in the nation."

Q "The dining halls, especially South, are really yummy compared to other places I've been. Also, **Recker's is wonderful anytime of day**, and if you're in the vicinity, the restaurant on the first floor of Grace Hall is good too."

The College Prowler Take On...
Campus Dining

In a darkened corner of Notre Dame's dining halls lurks a small section filled with the odor of ground mystery meat, fake taco shells, melted cheese, and shredded lettuce and tomato—the Mexican food section. It seems that not even this shadowy area of campus dining is lacking in student praise. Notre Dame students are very fond of their dining halls, particularly South, because of the variety of foods that they are able to find. Mexican, Chinese, Italian, and American food are just some of the choices available. And, while some students grow tired of the food selections in the dining halls, they find the small on-campus chain restaurants an equally appetizing 'Plan B.'

Although you may be able to predict the week's main food choices after a while, the contrasting food sections found in both North and South Dining Halls grant students the freedom of exploring their culinary creativity. Combined with the generous meal plans, which range from fourteen to twenty-one meals per week, meal points to use at campus restaurants and in vending machines, and the existence of 'Grab-N-Go' sack meals, the variety of food at the dining halls gives Notre Dame a grade that most cafeteria ladies can only dream about.

A

The College Prowler™ Grade on
Campus Dining: A

Our grade on Campus Dining addresses the quality of both school-owned dining halls and independent on-campus restaurants as well as the price, availability, and variety of food.

Off-Campus Dining

The Lowdown On...
Off-Campus Dining

Restaurant Prowler:
Popular Places to Eat!

Aunt Karen's Homestyle Deli
225 S. Michigan St.
Phone: (574) 232-8288

Boracho Burrito
1724 N. Ironwood Dr.
Phone: (574) 271-2033

Bruno's
2610 Prairie Ave.
Phone: (574) 288-3320

Buffalo Wild Wings
123 W Washington St
South Bend, IN 46601
Hours: Sunday 12pm-10pm;
Monday-Tuesday 11am-11pm;
Wednesday-Thursday 11am-
12am; Friday-Saturday
11am-1am
Phone: (574) 232-2293

BW-3
123 W. Washington St.
Phone: (574) 232-2293

Cambodian Eggroll
228 S. Michigan St.
Phone: (574) 289-2877

Catalino's Trattoria
235 S. Michigan St.
Phone: (574) 233-1000

Chicago Steak House
222 S. Michigan St.
Phone: (574) 234-5200

CJ's Pub
417 N. Michigan St.
Phone: (574) 233-5981

Famous Dave's BBQ
6402 Grape Rd. Mishawaka, IN
Phone: (574) 277-1188

The Fondue!
100 N. Center St.
Mishawaka, IN
Hours: Wednesday, Thursday:
5 p.m.-9 p.m.; Friday and
Saturday: 5 p.m.-10 p.m.

Golden Dragon
3302 Portage Ave.
Phone: (574) 243-8800

LaSalle Grill
115 W. Colfax Ave.
Hours: Monday-Thursday:
5 p.m.-10 p.m.; Friday and
Saturday: 5p.m.-11 p.m.
Phone: (574) 288-1155

Mandarin House Chinese Restaurant
2104 Edison Rd
South Bend, IN 46617
Hours: Sun-Thurs: 11 a.m.-8:45
p.m.Fri-Sat: 11 a.m.-9:45 p.m.
Phone: (574) 287-4414

Misty's Down Under
205 W. Jefferson Blvd.
Phone: (574) 234-4752

Original Pancake House (formerly Bibler's)
1430 N Ironwood Dr
South Bend, IN 46635
Hours: Everyday, 3 a.m.-2 p.m.
Phone: (574) 232-3220

Papa Vino's
5110 Edison Lakes Pkwy
Mishawaka, IN 46545
Hours: Sunday-Thursday:
11 a.m.-10 p.m.; Friday and
Saturday: 11 a.m.-11 p.m.
Phone: (574) 271-1692

Rib Shack
12613 Adams Rd. Granger, IN
Phone: (574) 277-3143

Rocco's Pizza
537 N. Saint Louis Blvd.
South Bend, IN 46617
Hours: Tuesday-Thursday: 5:00
p.m.-11:00 p.m.; Friday and
Saturday: 5:00 p.m.-1:00 a.m.
Phone: (574) 233-2464

Tippecanoe Place

620 W. Washington St.

Hours:

Brunch: Sunday: 9 a.m.-2 p.m.

Lunch: Monday-Friday: 11:30 a.m.-2 p.m.

Dinner: Monday-Friday: starting at 5 p.m.; Saturday: starting at 4:30 p.m.; Sunday: starting at 4:00 p.m.

Tom's Restaurant

131 S. Lafayette St.

Phone: (574) 237-9401

The Vine

123 S. Michigan St.

Phone: (574) 234-9463

Student Delivery Services:

Dine-In Delivery

11715 Mckinley Hwy

Osceola, IN

Hours:

Lunch: Monday-Friday 10AM-2PM

Dinner: Monday-Thursday 4PM-10PM; Friday 4PM-10:30PM; Saturday 3PM-10:30PM; Sunday 3PM-9PM

Phone: (574) 675-9999

www.dineinonline.com

Closest Grocery Store:

Meijer

5020 Grape Road

Mishawaka, IN 46545

Hours: Open 24 Hours a day

Phone: (574) 273-3506

Best Pizza:

Rocco's

Best Asian:

Mandarin House Chinese Restaurant

Best Breakfast:

Original Pancake House

Best Wings:

Buffalo Wild Wings

Best Place to Take Your Parents:

Papa Vino's

Students Speak Out On...
Off-Campus Dining

"There are many restaurants off-campus. South Bend is a college town that's geared toward students, parents and tourists."

Q "You have to have a car to get off-campus, but **there are a couple of places you can walk to if you are up for it**. Lula's is good for sandwiches and coffee, and there are a bunch of chain restaurants around too."

Q "Basically we have just about **every restaurant you can think of within ten minutes of campus**. The best spot would have to be Boracho Burrito. It's cheap and open until 4 a.m. for those drunken food cravings! It's only three blocks from the campus."

Q "**Morris Inn is the nicest restaurant on campus**. It has very good food. There are lots of places to go off-campus. Tippecanoe and La Salle Grill are good for expensive dining. For cheaper meals, there's BW3's, C.J.'s and The Vine, plus plenty of chains."

Q "South Bend is not that exciting of a city, but there are a few good restaurants around the area. First there are all your favorite chains: TGIFriday's, Applebee's, Chili's etc. Probably one of the most popular spots is called Papa Vino's, an Italian restaurant with fantastic food. All my guy friends think **Rocco's is the best pizza in town**—it's really good."

Q "If you want a fancy meal go to Tippecanoe Place. For those of age, **nothing beats a burger at C.J.'s pub**. Rocco's pizza is really good-especially when you're sick of Papa John's."

Q "Like any town, South Bend has fast food and places like The Olive Garden, Friday's, Chili's and Outback. There are also several good pizza places such as Bruno's, some Italian places like Papa Vino's, a few steak restaurants like The Rib Shack and Tippecanoe's, and oriental food at Mandarin House and Golden Dragon. **The phone book is chock full of fun places to eat**. While I haven't tried every place, I haven't had anything that wasn't good."

Q "All the restaurants are over on Grape Road, which isn't far. There are classics like The Olive Garden and Steak-n-Shake, but **my personal favorite is Famous Dave's BBQ–excellent!**"

Q "To be honest, the restaurants in South Bend are just like restaurants in any other town. **There aren't many good Mexican restaurants**, but what can you expect from the Midwest?"

Q "There are some pretty good places off-campus; **my favorite is Papa Vino's for a nicer environment with excellent pasta**. Then, there's Tippecanoe, which is an old mansion converted into a restaurant, and a Japanese hibachi/sushi restaurant with pretty good sushi. And finally, there's an Outback, a Lone Star Grill, a Steak-n-Shake, and an Olive Garden."

The College Prowler Take On...
Off-Campus Dining

While many say that a Notre Dame education will make a student a well-rounded person, students agree that an evening dining out in South Bend is not likely to be a cultural experience. Although there are a few unique places such as Fondue!, Tippecanoe, and a small Thai restaurant downtown, a night of off-campus dining is more likely to include dinner at one of the many chain restaurants that dominate the area. Students have, however, found a few non-chain restaurants that have become favorite places to eat the college staples of pizza, burgers, and late-night burritos, and they don't seem to mind too much that ethnic foods aren't in abundance.

The chain restaurant choices don't gain points, but student satisfaction with these restaurants helps to minimize any point deductions a bit. The services that accommodate students' appetites and lack of personal transportation—such as Dine-In Delivery—act as a plus, despite the estimated fifty to eighty-minute wait. Ultimately, even though the chain restaurants may make some feel at home, students are offered more variety at a lesser price in the dining hall.

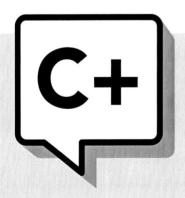

The College Prowler™ Grade on

Off-Campus Dining: C+

A high off-campus dining grade implies that off-campus restaurants are affordable, accessible, and worth visiting. Other factors include the variety of cuisine and the availability of alternative options (vegetarian, vegan, Kosher, etc.).

Campus Housing

The Lowdown On...
Campus Housing

Men's Halls:
Alumni Hall
Established: 1931

Mascot/Nickname: Dawgs

Colors: Green/White

Location: South Quad

Capacity: 269

Room Types: Singles, Doubles, Four-person Suites

Bathrooms: Community; private available in some suites

Signature event: The Wake

Carroll Hall
Established: Sold to Notre Dame in 1960 (previously a seminary)

Mascot/Nickname: Vermin

Colors: Scarlet/Gold

Location: South Quad

Capacity: 105

Room types: Singles, Doubles, Triples, Quads

Bathrooms: Community

Signature event: Carroll Christmas (Fall); Fusic Festival (Spring)

→

Dillon Hall
Established: 1931
Mascot/Nickname: Big Red
Colors: Red
Location: South Quad
Capacity: 338
Room types: Singles, Doubles, Triples, 3-person Suites, 4-person Suites
Bathrooms: Community; private available in some suites
Signature event: Dillon Pep Rally

Fisher Hall
Established: 1952
Mascot/Nickname: Green Wave
Colors: Green
Location: South Quad
Capacity: 189
Room types: Singles, Doubles, 4-person Suites
Bathrooms: Community; private available in some rooms
Signature event: Fisher Regatta

Keenan Hall
Established: 1957
Mascot/Nickname: Knights
Colors: Navy/White
Location: North Quad
Capacity: 293
Room types: Singles, Doubles
Bathrooms: Community
Signature event: Keenan Revue

Keough Hall
Established: 1996
Mascot/Nickname: Kangaroos
Colors: N/A
Location: West Quad
Capacity: 280
Room types: Singles, Doubles, Three-room Quads
Bathrooms: Community
Signature event: Keough Chariot Race

Knott Hall
Established: 1988
Mascot/Nickname: Juggerknotts
Colors: Orange
Location: Mod Quad
Capacity: 249
Room types: Singles, Doubles, Three-room Quads, One-room Triples
Bathrooms: Community
Signature event: Knott on the Knoll Concert

Morrissey Hall
Established: 1925
Mascot/Nickname: The Manor
Colors: Black/Gold
Location: South Quad
Capacity: 273
Room types: Singles, Doubles, Triples, Quads, 3-person Suites, 4-person Suites
Bathrooms: Community
Signature event: Morrissey Unplugged

O'Neil Hall

Established: 1996
Mascot/Nickname: The Mob
Colors: Blue/Gray
Location: West Quad
Capacity: 273
Room types: Singles, Doubles, Three-room Quads
Bathrooms: Community
Signature event: Mardi Gras

St. Edward's Hall

Established: 1882
Mascot/Nickname: N/A
Colors: Green/Gold
Location: North/God Quad
Capacity: 177
Room types: Doubles, Triples, 3-person Suites, 4-person Suites
Bathrooms: Community
Signature event: Founders Day and Founders Week Celebration

Siegfried Hall

Established: 1988
Mascot/Nickname: Ramblers
Colors: Maroon/Gray
Location: Mod Quad
Capacity: 249
Room types: Singles, Doubles, Three-room Quads, One-room Triples
Bathrooms: Community
Signature event: Rambler Scrambler

Sorin Hall

Established: 1888
Mascot/Nickname: Otters
Colors: N/A
Location: God Quad
Capacity: 154
Room types: Singles, Doubles, Triples, Quads, 3-person Suites, 4-person Suites
Bathrooms: Community
Signature event: Fall Talent Show

Stanford Hall

Established: 1957
Mascot/Nickname: Griffins
Colors: Green/Gold
Location: North Quad
Capacity: 278
Room types: Singles, Doubles, Triples
Bathrooms: Community
Signature event: Benefit

Zahm Hall

Established: 1937
Mascot/Nickname: Zahmbies
Colors: Red/Black
Location: North Quad
Capacity: 237
Room types: Singles, Doubles, Triples, 2-room Suites, 3-person Suites, 4-person Suites
Bathrooms: Community
Signature event: Winter Carnival

Women's Halls:

Badin Hall

Established: 1897

Mascot/Nickname: Bullfrogs

Colors: Green

Location: South Quad

Capacity: 124

Room types: Singles, Doubles, 4-person Suites

Bathrooms: Community

Signature event: Badin Spring Breakdown and Leprechaun Shakedown

Breen-Phillips

Established: 1939

Mascot/Nickname: Babes

Colors: Blue/Pink

Location: North Quad

Capacity: 210

Room types: Singles, Doubles, Triples, 4-person Suites

Bathrooms: Community

Signature event: BP Meal Auction for Charity

Cavanaugh Hall

Established: 1936

Mascot/Nickname: Chaos

Colors: Green

Location: North Quad

Capacity: 217

Room types: Singles, Doubles, 3-person Suites, 4-person Suites

Bathrooms: Community

Signature event: Women's Concerns; Snowball Dance

Farley Hall

Established: 1942

Mascot/Nickname: Finest

Colors: Green/Yellow

Location: North Quad

Capacity: 245

Room types: Singles, Doubles, 3-person Suites, 4-person Suites

Bathrooms: Community; private available in some rooms

Signature event: Pop Farley Week

Howard Hall

Established: 1924

Mascot/Nickname: Ducks

Colors: Yellow/Green

Location: South Quad

Capacity: 164

Room types: Singles, Doubles, Triples, 2-5 person Suites

Bathrooms: Community

Signature event: Campus-wide Marshmallow Roast; Howard Hoedown; Annual Bone Marrow Drive

Lewis Hall

Established: 1965

Mascot/Nickname: Chickens

Colors: Blue/Gold

Location: Between the Dome and St. Joe's Lake

Capacity: 294

Room types: Singles, Doubles, Triples, 4-person Suites

Bathrooms: Community

Signature event: N/A

Lyons Hall

Established: 1925
Mascot/Nickname: Lions
Colors: Black/Gold
Location: South Quad
Capacity: 211
Room types: Singles, Doubles, Triples, 2-person Suites, 3-person Suites, 4-person Suites
Bathrooms: Community; private available in some rooms
Signature event: Mara Fox Run

McGlinn Hall

Established: 1997
Mascot/Nickname: Shamrocks
Colors: Green
Location: West Quad
Capacity: 282
Room types: Singles, Doubles, 3-room Quads
Bathrooms: Community
Signature event: Casino Night

Pangborn Hall

Established: 1955
Mascot/Nickname: Phoxes
Colors: Purple/Green
Location: South Quad
Capacity: 179
Room types: Singles, Doubles, 4-person Suites, 6-person Suites
Bathrooms: Community; private bathrooms available for 6-person Suites
Signature event: Pangborn Price is Right; Phox Fire

Pasquerilla East

Established: 1981
Mascot/Nickname: Pyros
Colors: Red/Black
Location: Mod Quad
Capacity: 248
Room types: Singles, Doubles, 3-room Quads, 1-room Triples
Bathrooms: Community
Signature event: N/A

Pasquerilla West

Established: 1981
Mascot/Nickname: Purple Weasles
Colors: Purple
Location: Mod Quad
Capacity: 255
Room types: Singles, Doubles, 3-room Quads, One-room Triples
Bathrooms: Community

Walsh Hall

Established: 1909
Mascot/Nickname: Wild Women
Colors: Baby Blue/White
Location: God Quad
Capacity: 193
Room types: Singles, Doubles, Triples, 3-person Suites, 4-person Suites, 5-person Suites
Bathrooms: Community; private available in some suites
Signature event: Walsh Academy Fall Frolic

Welsh Family Hall
Established: 1997
Mascot/Nickname: Whirlwinds
Colors: Blue/White
Location: West Quad
Capacity: 267
Room types: Singles, Doubles, 3-room Quads
Bathrooms: Community
Signature event: Welsh Family Feud

Undergrads on Campus:
80%

Number of Dormitories:
27

Bed Type
Extra Long Twin

Room Types:
Single
Double
Triple
Quad
Suites (for 2-6 people)

Cleaning Service?
A cleaning service is available to clean the bathrooms, hallways and social space. Unless you request a repair in your room, maintenance will not enter student rooms.

What You Get
Each room is equipped with a bed, a desk a closet and a sink. The modern dorms have modular furniture, enabling students to easily create lofts. In addition, with the exception of some of the older dorms, most have laundry facilities.

Did You Know?

All residence halls at Notre Dame are single-sex.

The Main Building (also known as the Golden Dome) was originally intended to be used as a dorm.

"You have no choice on dorms, but they're all nice. If you get an older dorm, they have lots of tradition and a somewhat better atmosphere. If you get a newer dorm, they have air conditioning and the rooms are all a uniform size. The whole single-sex dorm issue is one of our favorite complaints as a student body."

"All the dorms are pretty nice. **There are newer dorms that are very nice**, but you have to be lucky to get into them. You get your own sink in your room, which is very convenient."

"You don't have a choice on the dorms, but generally **how much you like where you live depends more on who you live with**. Trust me, you can't avoid the people around your dorm. If you are around a bunch of backstabbers, you'll hate it no matter what. On the other hand, if you get paired with great people, you could live in a tent and love every minute."

"**You can't pick your dorm**. Some are nice and some suck; it's the luck of the draw. Each one has positives and negatives... you just have to deal with what you get."

"The dorms are alright–how much you'll enjoy them basically depends on who your rector is. My rector sucked, so I really didn't like my dorm too much, but **the majority of students truly love dorm life**. That's why 85% of students live on campus all four years."

Q "The dorms are all very unique. The older dorms have a lot of tradition. People **develop a lot of bias towards their dorms**, so I'll automatically tell you that mine is the best."

Q "The new dorms have air conditioning, but **they're all identical**. Personally, I wouldn't want to live there."

Q "All of the thirty or so dorms are unique and each dorm community has its own personality. The older dorms are overflowing with school pride and tradition, and the **newer dorms are the most accommodating, hold the most students, and make for bigger, more diverse communities**. Many athletes also choose to reside in the newer dorms, so if you are a resident of one of the newer dorms, be ready to rub elbows with many of the star athletes on campus."

Q "All the dorms are nice. **Zahm, Cavanaugh, Farley, Alumni and others provide a history and a comfy brick feeling**. Knott, O'Neil, McGlinn and others are newer, have air conditioning, and are more modern."

Q "Freshmen do not have a choice on their dorm or their roommate. So, good luck. **As a sophomore, you get to pick both your dorm and your roommates**."

Q "**The dorms are the true heart of Notre Dame**. I don't know that there are particular dorms to avoid-you'll be told that Zahm is a horrible place to live and that it isn't one of the wildest dorms on campus, but it also has a lot of camaraderie and the Zahmies really take care of each other. Dillon and Alumni have a lot of history, but their facilities aren't as nice."

Q "**The dorms vary.** I got lucky and was put into one of the newest dorms on-campus, Welsh Fam. It's great–our rooms are huge, we've got air conditioning, and I ended up with some really great roommates for next year."

The College Prowler Take On...
Campus Housing

Ah , dorm life: finding food in strange places; living so close to your neighbor that you can actually hear them snore; dealing with the constant presence of a roommate's significant other; avoiding the rector at all costs; wearing a dorm shirt every time you're out of clean clothes. Students agree that no Notre Dame education would be complete without a stay in the dorms. Freshmen are not allowed to pick either their dorm or their roommates, but the majority feel that the university does a fairly good job in making the final decision. If a student is unhappy with the dorm in which they were placed, they have the freedom to be pulled into another dorm or to move off-campus after they reach their sophomore year. There are twenty-seven dorms on campus, and all are single-sex and subject to parietals, which are the only hours when members of the opposite sex are allowed to visit. Of the twenty-seven dorms, the're no clear student preference. While the older dorms seem to be favored by some because of their traditions, the luxury and comfort of the newer dorms are preferred by others. Whether old or new, student pride runs rampant throughout the dorms.

B

The College Prowler™ Grade on
Campus Housing: B

A high Campus Housing grade indicates that dorms are clean, well-maintained, and spacious. Other determining factors include variety of dorms, proximity to classes, and social atmosphere.

Off-Campus Housing

The Lowdown On...
Off-Campus Housing

Undergrads in Off-Campus Housing:
20%

Average Rent for a Studio:
$475

Average Rent for a 1BR:
$550

Average Rent for a 2BR:
$625

For Assistance Contact:
See "Off-campus housing information" at Notre Dame's website. Related links can also be found there, such as Realtor.com and SouthBend.com.

Popular Areas:

Turtle Creek Apartments

1710 Turtle Creek Drive
South Bend, IN
(574) 272-8124

Castle Point Apartments

18011 Cleveland
South Bend, IN
(574) 272-8110

College Park Apartments

18083 Bulla
South Bend, IN
(574) 272-0691

Best Time to Look for a Place:

At least a year in advance

Students Speak Out On...
Off-Campus Housing

"You have to live on-campus your freshman year, but it's not a big deal, since many students stay on-campus all four years. There are several apartment complexes within a half-mile from campus where many students live."

"Off-campus housing is excellent. **Lots of parties, cheap rent and lots of 'student only' housing complexes**."

"Some housing is really close—within walking distance—but those aren't that nice. The **farther you get from campus, the nicer the housing**. Everyone lives on-campus for at least two years; most people for three. I'll be a senior living on-campus next semester and that's very typical—probably half of the seniors live on-campus."

"The most popular place to live off-campus is Turtle Creek apartments. They are the closest, and they have the most parties. **It's also popular to get a house with a bunch of people on the streets surrounding the campus**. Honestly, though, most people like living on-campus. If they do move, it's not until senior year. Dorm life is really great."

"Forget living off-campus freshman year. Besides the fact that you aren't allowed to do it, it's also not very convenient. **There is one apartment complex next to campus, and it's not bad, but every student is trying for a place there**, so most of the apartments are taken up by upperclassmen. I lived on-campus all four years, and for what it's worth, I think it's the best route to go."

Q "**It is not very convenient**, and you probably won't ever move off-campus."

Q "It's good, **but it's broken into much more often**."

Q "Off-campus housing is hardly as academically convenient as living on-campus. There are apartments located near campus, but you still need a vehicle to get from there to campus, and you need to book your apartment two years in advance! Living off-campus is also a big risk because **most of the student houses are located in the bad part of town**. I've heard horror stories of students having to deal with the locals and having their houses robbed when they go away for breaks."

Q "My feeling is that **if you like your dorm, stay there!** Living off-campus is a fine alternative, but there is so much you can get from dorm life."

The College Prowler Take On...
Off-Campus Housing

The freedoms to yell at all hours of the night, to party whenever you want and—perhaps most importantly—to have a significant other spend the night all make off-campus living immediately appealing. However, the fact that eighty percent of the student population is fond enough of campus life to remain there for at least three, and more than likely all four years, says much about where student preference lies. Nevertheless, those who choose to live off-campus say that the apartment complexes are pretty close to campus and fairly well-kept. Although there may be a higher incidence of crime, and some off-campus houses may be in sketchy areas, such factors do not push these students back into the dorms.

Despite the fact that many students who move off-campus are happy with their apartments, the massive amount of students who choose to remain on-campus for at least three years indicates that, while it may have some advantages, there is nothing particularly special about off-campus housing. Students enjoy going to off-campus parties, but they also mention how off-campus housing is vulnerable to crime, especially in certain areas of South Bend.

The College Prowler™ Grade on

Off-Campus Housing: C+

A high grade in Off-Campus Housing indicates that apartments are of high quality, close to campus, affordable, and easy to secure.

Diversity

The Lowdown On...
Diversity

American Indian:
Less than 1%

**Asian or
Pacific Islander:**
5%

African American:
4%

Hispanic:
8%

White:
79%

International:
5%

Out of State:
Over 50%

➜

Gay Tolerance:

Gay tolerance is promoted by The Standing Committee on Gay and Lesbian Student Needs

Most Popular Religions:

Catholicism

Economic Status:

Generally Upper-Middle to Upper Class

Political Activity:

There are ten official political organizations on campus. These include:

• Social Action Club
• Amnesty International
• Campus Alliance for Rape Elimination
• East Timor Action Network
• ND for Animals
• Pax Christi
• Progressive Student Alliance
• Right to Life
• Student Environmental Action
• Women's Resource Center

Minority Clubs:

There are 22 ethnic and cultural organizations. These are:

• Asian American Association
• Asian International Society
• Australia Club
• Black Cultural Arts Council
• Brazil Club
• Caribbean Student Organization
• Filipino Club
• Gaelic Society
• German Club
• Hawaii Club
• India Association
• International Student Organization
• Italian Club
• Japan Club
• Korean Student Association
• La Allianza
• Le Cercle Franais (the French Club)
• NAACP
• Polish Club
• Russian Club
• Spanish Club
• Vietnamese Student Association

Students Speak Out On...
Diversity

"It's not too diverse. I mean, there are the typical Irish-Catholic students who are probably the majority here, but there aren't many different minorities. We're getting better about it, and we have a lot of groups that have made names for themselves."

Q "**Notre Dame is not very diverse**. White and Catholic is the majority."

Q "Notre Dame is **overwhelmingly white and Catholic**."

Q "Not too diverse, though the school claims otherwise. **It's definitely dominated by white Americans**."

Q "Notre Dame is always trying to improve on the diversity of its students, but **the campus could be much more diverse**. I came from a very diverse high school, so I was not used to the lack of diversity. If I had one complaint about Notre Dame this would probably be it. I cannot think of one person on campus that is closed-minded about it though."

Q "Everyone looks alike! Well, not exactly, but the majority are white and upper class. It's difficult to find minorities, but I think the school is trying to work on that. I wish it was more diverse, because **all the preppy people get on my nerves sometimes**."

Q "Diversity is definitely a weak point, but they're working to improve it. **Multi-cultural events are very popular**."

Q "ND is fairly homogenous, with the majority of people being Caucasian Catholics. You will certainly find many people from other minority groups who are very happy at ND. I also know that to some people, **Notre Dame can be intimidating**. I certainly hope that no one feels that they are not welcome to attend Notre Dame because of their race/ethnicity."

Q "Notre Dame is smack dab in the middle of the Midwest, so it's no surprise to find that a vast majority of students are Caucasian. Black and Hispanic communities are small, but growing and very supportive. There is also a noticeable international student population. Racism is not present anywhere on-campus, but **there are students who have never encountered people from other cultures and are not as understanding** as others. Don't be intimidated by the lack of diversity though. Be yourself, and people will accept you, regardless of race."

Q "I would say relatively diverse, but it seriously lacks the percentage of under-represented minority students. **The campus has improved in this arena**, but it still has a long way to go. Stereotypes are still alive and well and the general population needs to be educated about other cultures, races and ethnicities."

Q "If you're white and Catholic, or you like white Catholics, **you'll do fine**."

The College Prowler Take On...
Diversity

If Notre Dame wanted to change its mascot, it could replace the fighting leprechaun with a white kid wearing a crucifix—roughly eighty percent of the student population is white and Catholic. Nevertheless, the University is continuously attempting to reach out and attract minority students. Quite a few minority students do choose to attend Notre Dame, and many minority groups band together in alliances that act as celebrations of ethnicity. While these events are popular and promote ethnic understanding among students, everyone agrees that the University is trudging along a long and winding road to diversity.

At Notre Dame, the ratio of white students to minority students is 35:1. This lack of diversity is one of Notre Dame's greatest weaknesses. No matter how diligently the university wrestles with this weakness, its success in attracting minority students has always been marginal. Although Notre Dame is not a campus that promotes discrimination, many non-white students may sometimes feel out of place. The ethnic alliances provide minority students with some comfort, but, despite this, the university receives low marks for diversity.

The College Prowler™ Grade on

Diversity: D-

A high grade in Diversity indicates that ethnic minorities and international students have a notable presence on campus and that students of different economic backgrounds, religious beliefs, and sexual preferences are well-represented.

Guys & Girls

The Lowdown On...
Guys & Girls

Men Undergrads:
52%

Women Undergrads:
48%

Birth Control Available?
No.

Did You Know?

According to Notre Dame legend, the first person who walks with you around the lakes, goes to the Grotto with you, or kisses you under the arch at Lyons Hall is the person that you will marry.

Top Places to find Hotties:
• At a party / bar
• At one of the gyms
• In the dining hall

Hookups or Relationships?
Although relationships do occur, hookups are the most frequent and noticeable on campus.

Best Place to Meet Guys/Girls:
• Parties/Bars
• Class

Dress Code
Notre Dame's school newspaper, The Observer, once featured an article discussing the student's unofficial dress code. In this article, the author outlined the image of the average ND student: designer jeans, crew neck sweaters, leather jackets, pea coats, and shoulder strap back packs. The fact is that a walk through campus can often feel like a glimpse through the latest J. Crew catalog. Although there are a few brave souls who dare to make unique fashion statements, the majority of the Notre Dame community opts for a casual conservative look on a daily basis. However, when the lights go down, the party comes alive with students ditching the confines of preppiness for a much more outgoing—and sometimes revealing—look.

Students Speak Out On...
Guys & Girls

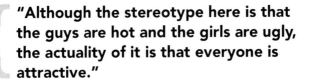

{ **"Although the stereotype here is that the guys are hot and the girls are ugly, the actuality of it is that everyone is attractive."**

Q "You will be disappointed with Notre Dame if you're going to college for a great or liberal social scene. There are **lots of very old-school Catholic people**, and many do not care about their looks."

Q "The dating scene is **really, really weak** at Notre Dame."

Q "As a guy, I can say that most guys are pretty good looking. A survey from somewhere ranked Notre Dame as the third best school for guys. As far as girls, I think they were at 163 or something. There are some very nice girls and a couple of attractive girls, but **if you are looking for cute girls go somewhere else**."

Q "The guys are hot, and the girls are really pretty. At this campus, **people dress up to go to classes**–it's really funny actually; I mean, there are times when I'll go to class in warm-up pants and a sweatshirt, but there are always people in really trendy, dressy clothes."

Q "There are lots of guys, **no matter what your taste is**."

Q "I have met some incredible people here that are my best friends and will be forever, but there will be people that you don't like too. I always complain that **everyone is so conformist** that they look like they fell out of an Abercrombie and Fitch catalog."

Q "A lot of ND guys complain about the girls, but it's not really that bad. With single sex dorms and parietals-rules about when members of the opposite sex can be in the dorms, **relations between the sexes are notoriously bad**; but it's really up to you. I think it's mostly a cop-out for people who can't meet people. I've met plenty of attractive females. And you'd have to ask the girls about how hot we guys are."

Q "Females in general, at Notre Dame, have to be some of the most underdressed women on the planet. Some of them don't even wear makeup! Some of them don't even shave! Talk about a lack of eye-candy. It's a sad thing. **You can really tell that the majority of the females at ND are total bookworms and are only here for the academics**. Cosmopolitan magazine really needs to visit Notre Dame and give the girls on campus a serious make over! If you're able to find yourself a good- looking keeper, you're definitely a lucky man."

Q "Bad news, here: **the average ND girl is uptight** and, well… most of them aren't very fun. Don't get me wrong, there are some gorgeous girls at school. I know all of them...and so do most of the football players, so kiss them goodbye."

Q "There are 8,000 undergrads at ND, so there's someone for everyone. **The dating scene is a little skewed because of parietals**, which are hours when girls must leave guys' dorms and vice versa, but it is there and regardless of your dating status, you'll have a great time with all your new friends."

Q "**The hotness of the guys at Notre Dame is almost mythical**. Students joke around that some girls attend Notre Dame because they know that the guys are smart AND hot. High school girls even take campus tours just so that they can look at all the hot guys, and sometimes they even bring their cameras so that they can take pictures of them. No joke!."

Q "Both the guys and girls are pretty attractive. But the dating scene is bizarre. **It seems that either people hook up or are in serious relationships**, but you find very few people in between. Whoever figures out how to change this could make a lot of money."

The College Prowler Take On...
Guys & Girls

Both the dating scene and male-female relations at Notre Dame are seriously different from many other schools you may look at—especially large, public schools or schools in more urban settings. With single-sex dorms and parietals firmly in place, guys and girls are kept apart from the beginning, and largely tend to stay that way. With the exception of group projects, nights out, or the rare couple that is actually dating, members of the opposite sex don't interact often; typically, anyone who walks through the student center can see groups of guys and girls in distinctly different places—kind of like those dances you used to go to in middle school.

Although female students rated the guys at Notre Dame quite highly, men did not have quite the same praise for the girls. The stereotypical Notre Dame guy is both intelligent and hot, while girls apparently run the gamut from "uptight" to simply unattractive. It's likely you'll find plenty of exceptions to both of these standards, however. While the Notre Dame social scene is quite skewed, it hasn't been pronounced dead on arrival—you will see the occasional serious couple walking arm-in-arm, and hookups are not really uncommon.

The College Prowler™ Grade on
Guys: B+

A high grade for Guys indicates that the male population on campus is attractive, smart, friendly, and engaging, and that the school has a decent ratio of guys to girls.

The College Prowler™ Grade on
Girls: C+

A high grade for Girls not only implies that the women on campus are attractive, smart, friendly, and engaging, but also that there is a fair ratio of girls to guys.

Athletics

The Lowdown On...
Athletics

Athletic Division:
NCAA Division 1

Conference:
Independent (football)
Big East (other sports)

Men's Varsity Sports:
Baseball
Basketball
Cross-Country
Fencing

Men's Varsity Sports (continued):
Football
Golf
Ice Hockey
Lacrosse
Soccer
Swimming
Tennis
Track and Field

Men Playing Varsity Sports:
476 (4%)

→

Women's Varsity Sports:

Basketball
Cross-Country
Fencing
Golf
Lacrosse
Rowing
Soccer
Softball
Swimming
Tennis
Track and Field
Volleyball

Women Playing Varsity Sports:

294 (6%)

Club Sports:

Aikido
Bowling
Climbing
Cycling
Equestrian
Field Hockey
Figure Skating
Fly Fishing
Gymnastics
Martial Arts
Men's Boxing
Men's Rowing
Men's Running

Club Sports (continued):

Men's Volleyball
Men's Water Polo
Pom Pom Squad
Rodeo
Sailing
Skiing
Ultimate Frisbee
Women's Boxing
Women's Ice Hockey
Women's Running
Women's Water Polo
World Tae Kwan Do
Federation

Intramurals:

Badminton
Baseball
Basketball
Broomball
Cross-Country
Football
Golf
Hockey
Horseshoes
Lacrosse
Raquetball
Soccer
Squash
Table Tennis
Tennis
Ultimate Frisbee
Volleyball
Water Polo

Athletic Fields:

- Notre Dame Stadium
- Frank Eck Stadium
- Ivy Field
- Moose Krause Stadium
- Alumni Field
- Loftus Sports Center

School Mascot:
Fighting Irish

Most Popular Sports
Football and Basketball

Overlooked Teams:
Baseball and Cross-Country

Best Place to Take a Walk
Around the lakes

Getting Tickets
Season tickets are available to all students. Students are notified about ticket availability and purchasing times via email.

Gyms/Facilities:
Joyce Center

The Joyce Center (JACC) plays a variety of roles. It's well-used for both varsity sports and commercial events, yet it's also a well-equipped gym. Included among the facilities are five courts for basketball and volleyball, four racquetball courts, faculty fitness and locker rooms, an ice rink, jogging lanes, a varsity shop, and boxing rooms. However, the JACC's use for varsity sports and events leaves limited hours for recreational availability. Unless they have an athletic class in this building, most students prefer to workout elsewhere.

Knute Rockne Memorial

Affectionately known as "the Rock," this facility is dedicated to the memory of Notre Dame football coach Knute Rockne. The lower level is recently renovated, and building amenities include a fitness room with cardio and select weight equipment, a weight room, two courts for basketball and volleyball, a 25-yard pool and shallow exercise pool, activity rooms for fitness and dance classes, and a climbing wall. Although the Rock is well-equipped, most students find its gothic architecture discomforting. Overall, the Rock is not a social gym.

Rolf's Aquatic Center

Rolf's Sport Recreation Center is the University's newest recreation facility, and by far the most popular. It houses a fitness room with cardio and strength-training equipment, three courts for basketball, volleyball, and badminton, a multi-purpose court for soccer, handball, in-line hockey, lacrosse, and volleyball, an 1/8-mile suspended running track, pool tables and table tennis, activity rooms for fitness and dance classes, and the Health and Fitness Resource Center. With its state-of-the-art facilities and social environment, Rolf's is the perfect place to go for fitness or otherwise.

Also Available:
• Eck Tennis Pavilion
• Courtney Tennis Center
• Warren Golf Course

Students Speak Out On...
Athletics

"Varsity sports are life at Notre Dame. Intramurals are also very prominent and very fun."

Q "You won't find another university in America with better intramurals. **Sports dominate the social scene at Notre Dame.**"

Q "**Varsity sports, especially football, are very big**, and it's fun to see everyone get so excited about them."

Q "Varsity and intramural sports are both huge! Football dominates the fall semester. Everyone gets wasted before the games on Saturday. **Intramurals are big**, especially when the dorms compete against each other."

Q "**Huge**. That's all I'm going to say."

Q "Notre Dame is a pretty big athletic school. Varsity athletics are big on campus. **There's nothing like a Notre Dame football weekend, even if you aren't a football fan**. Besides the varsity sports, there are also several club sports and countless intramurals. The intramurals become a great way to socialize and can be very competitive."

Q "Huge—Notre Dame is one of the top jock schools in the country. Football games are all-day events; it's a lot of fun and everyone goes. It's huge. Most of the competition for intramural sports can be seen in inter-hall games. You place for your residence hall and there are some fierce rivalries, especially in dorm football. **Notre Dame is the only school that plays intramural tackle football**."

Q "Sports are huge at ND. Hello, we are the Fighting Irish! Football rules, by far. Varsity sports are huge, and so are IM sports. Most students were involved in athletics in high school, so they continue them in some form at ND. I played IM soccer and I loved it! **You make so many more friends and it's good competition**, but at a level that the normal ND student can handle."

Q "Varsity sports are HUGE. Football, of course, rules the fall. **IM football is a lot of fun to both play and watch**. If football isn't your thing, there are tons of other activities that lots of people get involved in. Anything you want to get involved in you can either find or start up yourself."

Q "Come on, this is Notre Dame! Football practically has its own religious denomination on campus. **If you're a varsity athlete, you are worshipped and loved by everyone**. The reason for this is because, overall, Notre Dame students are extremely athletic and know what it takes to be a varsity athlete."

The College Prowler Take On...
Athletics

It looks like the term "Fighting Irish" might be an understatement. Whether it's on the playing field or in the stands, Notre Dame students love a good fight. Sports are a part of the Notre Dame tradition. Most students play sports, have played sports, love sports, or are learning to love them here. Whether varsity or intramural, students flock to watch and participate in Notre Dame athletics. With varsity sports ranging from water polo to football, and IM sports including figure skating and basketball, there's certainly much more to do here than study.

If Notre Dame wasn't a Catholic university, it would be religiously affiliated with sports. Notre Dame is the epitome of the college athletic tradition. Students here do not sit during football or basketball games. They bathe themselves in Kelly-green paint, spell out IRISH on bared bodies, and will spend four hours standing in the snow to watch the Fighting Irish play. And believe me, they'll play anything. From inter-hall football to horseshoes, there's a sport for anyone willing to participate. The spirit, determination, student participation, and the expansive program vaults Notre Dame's athletics into a champion's spot.

The College Prowler™ Grade on

Athletics: A

A high grade in Athletics indicates that students have school spirit, that sports programs are respected, that games are well-attended, and that intramurals are a prominent part of student life.

Nightlife

The Lowdown On...
Nightlife

Club and Bar Prowler:
Popular Nightlife Spots!

Club Prowler:
Boat Club, Inc.

106 N. Hill St.

(574) 288-6888

Boat Club was a strong student favorite due to their supposed liberal policy on carding. It was alleged that this policy is what led to the closing of the club, however, and their present status is unknown.

Club 23

744 N. Notre Dame Ave.

(574) 234-4015

Heartland

222 S. Michigan St.

(574) 234-5200

Students say that Heartland is the closest thing to a dance club that South Bend offers.

Bar Prowler:
Benchwarmer's Sports Lounge

236 S. Michigan St.

(574) 232-0022

→

Bootlegger's
1302 Ford St.
(574) 234-4215

Busby's Tavern
805 Lincoln Way W.
(574) 233-0988

CJ's Pub
417 N. Michigan St.
(574) 233-5981

Corby's Irish Pub
441 E. LaSalle Ave.
(574) 233-5326

Frank's Place
327 W. Marion St.
(574) 232-2277

Fiddler's Hearth
127 N. Main St.
(574) 232-2853

GloWorm Lounge
720 S.Michigan St.
(574) 237-9161

Library Irish Club
113 E. Wayne St.
(574) 283-0452

Linebacker Lounge
1631 S. Bend Ave.
(574) 289-0186

Bars Close At:
2 a.m.

Favorite Drinking Games:
Beer Pong
Card Games
(A$$hole, Ride the Bus)
Quarters
Power Hour

Student Favorites
Boat Club
Heartland
The Library/Finnegan's
C.J.'s

Useful Resources for Nightlife
True to form, cabbies usually know what the hot spots are for the evening. Otherwise, the bar scene is most prevalent during the week, and off-campus parties dominate the weekends. It's all a matter of knowing people.

What to Do if You're Not 21
If you're not 21, you are always more than welcome at dorm parties and off-campus house parties. For those who are not too fond of drinking, the Student Union Board usually sponsors weekend movies, and there is an alcohol-free group called Flipside that has weekly events.

Students Speak Out On...
Nightlife

"Parties are okay on-campus. After a while, the scene gets old. The bars off-campus are okay. Heartland was the place to be on Thursday nights. The Linebacker was good on Friday or Saturday, especially during home games."

"The parties on-campus can be fun, but the excitement wears off after a year or so. It's a great way to meet people as a freshman. If I can give one piece of advice it would be to **go to parties as a freshman, even if you don't drink**. You will find that you are definitely not the only one. Don't think that if you don't drink people won't hang out with you. Off-campus, I really like C.J.'s and Corby's."

"**I have two words for you: Boat Club!** I don't think that anyone that goes there is actually 21, but it's definitely a favorite bar for the freshmen and sophomores. That's probably because it's so easy to get in!"

"Bars. Okay, in South Bend you have to be 21 to get into bars, so, technically, you won't be frequenting those... that said, fake IDs are very prevalent on campus. As a freshman, if you have a fake or if you borrow one, you will undoubtedly go to Boat Club–the place is disgusting! **There are a lot of places to go, but you have to be prepared**. I know some people who have gotten busted for fake IDs, and that's not good because it can affect your ability to study abroad."

"Nightlife is great when you're 21 or have a good fake. **There are no real clubs, but lots of bars**."

"If you're 21, Heartland is your best bet. If not, you have to settle for a couple of dive bars, but they are all very fun. **Off-campus parties are the center of party life**."

"Students go to a lot of bars, but **mostly there are dorm parties since we're allowed to have alcohol in our dorms**. Also, there are a lot of parties at the apartment complexes off-campus."

"**South Bend has plenty of bars and clubs**. Boat Club is the biggest bar for underage people because you can get away with fake IDs there, but most of the bars and clubs are for people 21 and older."

"The club scene is non-existent, unless you want to drive 10 miles to Elkhart, The bars are a lot of fun. They range from the friendly Boat Club to Heartland, which is the closest thing to a dance club. **Each bar has its own identity**, which is cool."

"On-campus parties can be fun, but don't compare to the off-campus version. Bars and **off-campus parties are usually the way to go**. McCormick's and the Library are great places to check out. Boat Club was the place to go if you wanted a trashy joint, cheap beer and freshman girls, but it got shut down for alcohol violations. We're hoping they'll re-open as a sweet new bar."

The College Prowler Take On...
Nightlife

The student consensus is that campus parties are the way to go during your first year. Once they lose their appeal, as they inevitably do, parties at apartment complexes and student houses take preference. The club scene is relatively weak, leaving students to choose from a limited variety of bars.

At Notre Dame, students study hard and party hard. The allowance of alcohol in student rooms enables students to make any night a party night. However, the relatively small number of bars combined with the lack of a good club scene is a drawback of Notre Dame nightlife. Overall, the party scene here is the same as most places: there are plenty of good times available if you know where to go. And students advise knowing where to go; a few years ago, there were rumors of a group of freshmen who, looking very chic, wandered in to their first off-campus party; it turned out to be a high-school party! Yes, I'd say that knowing where to go is a definite plus.

B-

The College Prowler™ Grade on
Nightlife: B-

A high grade in Nightlife indicates that there are many bars and clubs in the area that are easily accessible and affordable. Other determining factors include the number of options for the under-21 crowd and the prevalence of house parties.

Greek Life

The Lowdown On...
Greek Life

Number of Fraternities:
0

Number of Sororities:
0

Students Speak Out On...
Greek Life

> "We don't have Greek life. Our dorms are single-sex, though, so they are sort of like our houses in a sense. I don't feel like I'm missing out on anything."

Q "**There is no Greek life on-campus, which actually makes for a great atmosphere**, in my opinion. Many people comment on how the dorms act as their own sororities or fraternities, which in many ways is true. Dorms compete against each other in events, like the Late Night Olympics and intramural sports, and they have their own signature dances. Walsh Hall's most famous event is the Fall Frolic, a dance where we all dress up like Catholic schoolgirls. It's lots of fun. If you ask anyone on-campus, they will than likely say that their dorm is the best on campus. However, this 'dorm pride' doesn't overwhelm resident life."

Q "There are no frats at ND. **They try to have the dorm life take the place of Greek life,** but it really does not compare."

Q "**You identify with your dorm**. Most people live at the same one all their years on-campus. There are dorm dances, sports, and activities. It's a great system. I think it's better and more inclusive than any Greek system I've heard of."

Q "In a way, the dorms have become a Greek system, but **you can choose to be as involved or uninvolved as you like**. No one would judge you for it the way they would in a sorority or fraternity."

Q "No Greeks. Instead, the campus is dominated by the residential system. The dorms act as fraternities or sororities. In my opinion, **you get all the great stuff without the egos or the hazing**."

Q "Notre Dame has no Greek system, but it really doesn't matter because, **with all the competitiveness and dorm spirit that all the dorms have, you don't really notice**."

Q "ND doesn't have sororities/fraternities, but each dorm does basically have the same sports, dances/mixers, charity events, and campus wide functions, so **you only miss out on paying the huge sorority dues**!"

Q "We don't have Greek life, which is really nice. **There aren't any stereotypes like on many other campuses**. There are times when I wish I DID have Greek life, but they're mostly when I'm talking to my friends at home who are in sororities. The way I look at it is, I don't miss what I've never had, but I HAVE had a great time with my friends without Greek life."

Q "There is no Greek life at ND, but in its place is an incredible dorm spirit. The dorm gives you everything and more that a fraternity or sorority would. **When you meet an alumnus, the first question is always 'What dorm did you live in?'** It really has a huge impact on life at Notre Dame."

The College Prowler Take On...
Greek Life

There are no Greek life divisions at Notre Dame, and most students don't miss them too much. Although there's no way to contrast life at Notre Dame with life in a sorority or fraternity, students agree that the dorm atmosphere is a nice substitute that lacks none of the Greek flavoring. Dorm pride allows for friendly rivalries and makes up for the lack of fraternity/sorority "cliques," and there are plenty of residence hall activities that mirror what you'll find in most Greek houses.

The College Prowler™ Grade on

Greek Life: N/A

A high grade in Greek Life indicates that sororities and fraternities are not only present, but also active on campus. Other determining factors include the variety of houses available and the respect the Greek community receives from the rest of the campus.

Drug Scene

The Lowdown On...
Drug Scene

Liquor-Related Referrals:
127

Liquor-Related Arrests:
69

Drug-Related Referrals:
1

Drug-Related Arrests:
6

Most Prevalent Drugs on Campus:
Alcohol
Marijuana

Drug Counseling Programs:
Drug counseling services are available through the student Health Center and the Office of Alcohol and Drug Education. For more information on these services, contact the Office of Alcohol and Drug Education located at 311 La Fortune Student Center or call: (574) 631-7970

Students Speak Out On...
Drug Scene

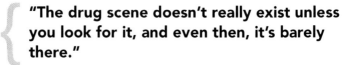

{ **"The drug scene doesn't really exist unless you look for it, and even then, it's barely there."**

Q "My experience is that there is more of it going on than the school cares to admit. **No one talks about it, but it is definitely around**. You can avoid it easily or get into it easily, whichever you want."

Q "There's very little drug use to speak of. If you want drugs, I guess it's not too hard to find them, but **alcohol is, by far, the drug of choice**."

Q "The only drug I know that anyone uses is marijuana, and that's **not real common**."

Q "There's a lot of drinking here, but **drugs are rare**."

Q "The drug scene really **depends on who you hang out with**."

Q "Drugs certainly aren't prominent, but don't be fooled. **They're here**."

Q "There are pretty much no drugs on campus. **Some weed, but that's about it**. I've never seen any real drug problems."

Q "Mostly, I've seen weed, but I know there's other stuff, too. **You can get kicked out if you are caught with drugs**."

Q "While there is an **occasional isolated flare-up** of drug use on campus, there is absolutely no tolerance of this by the administration. Being caught means immediate expulsion."

Q "It exists, but you have to look for it. Here, **booze is the mind-altering drug of choice**."

The College Prowler Take On...
Drug Scene

If you happen to be walking around campus one day and spot a thin, pale, haggard-looking teen, don't panic. At Notre Dame, the sight of such a person is more likely to indicate that they're an Architecture major overdosing on coffee at the end of an all-nighter, rather than strung out. Across the board students say that, while drugs are available around campus, they're the exception rather than the rule. Although alcohol can be found in excess, the university's strict zero-tolerance drug policy seems to be frightening enough to check the few students who are even interested in drug use.

Needless to say, you don't have to worry about social pressure to use drugs at Notre Dame. Whatever does happen is always in isolated circles, and punishments can be so serious that drugs tend to stay out of sight. Of course there are things around – this is the case at any campus. But Notre Dame is not the type of school where you can toke up every day and still expect to graduate.

A-

The College Prowler™ Grade on

Drug Scene: A-

A high grade in the Drug Scene indicates that drugs are not a noticeable part of campus life; drug use is not visible, and no pressure to use them seems to exist.

Campus Strictness

The Lowdown On...
Campus Strictness

What Are You Most Likely to Get Caught Doing on Campus?

- Sex
- Drug use/possession
- Sex

Students Speak Out On...
Campus Strictness

"The drinking policy on-campus is pretty lenient. In a way, it teaches you to be responsible in a safe environment where an RA is always available to help. The drug policy is very strict, but I don't know anyone that has gotten in trouble or could have reason to worry."

Q "There is **absolutely no tolerance for drugs**. Drinking, on the other hand, is fairly open with some limitations. If you are a responsible drinker and are respectful to yourself and to those around you, you will have no problem with drinking on-campus (behind closed doors, of course)."

Q "Getting caught with drugs means immediate expulsion. Drinking isn't taken as seriously as drugs, unless you're stupidly drunk and falling all over yourself. The only advice I have is to not get idiotically drunk and campus police won't bother you. Being the most famous of Catholic institutions, and therefore the strictest, **getting caught having sex on-campus will get you kicked off-campus**. Be smart and be cautious if you're ever going to fool around."

Q "Notre Dame is **not very strict concerning drinking.** We are one of the few campuses that allow beer in the dorms. Hard alcohol was recently banned, but students have it anyway."

Q "The campus is getting stricter about drinking – no hard alcohol is allowed in the dorms, but you are allowed to have beer and other alcohol in your room if you are 21. This policy is never enforced, so, **basically, you can have alcohol whenever you want**."

Q "They're trying to crack down on drinking now. We'll see how this goes. **Notre Dame students study very hard and party hard as well.** Drugs are completely out. I don't know many people that do them and I wouldn't advise it. While Notre Dame might be lax on underage drinking, they have absolutely no tolerance for drugs."

Q "We do not have a dry campus at Notre Dame, **so drinking is allowed in the dorms**! Hard alcohol isn't allowed in the dorms anymore because of too many cases of alcohol poisoning, but you can still have beer. And, really, how will they know if you do have hard alcohol?"

Q "You can have parties in your dorm with beer and so forth, but you can't have people throwing up in the hall. **It's lax compared to lots of schools.**"

Q "They're **very strict on drugs, but not on drinking**."

Q "**If you get caught, you basically just have to do community service**–they're not too bad about stuff."

Q "The drinking policy is very lax. **It's okay to drink in your room no matter what age, as long as you have the door closed**. Off-campus parties are big and loud, but if they're broken up it's usually later in the evening. There isn't much of a drug scene, but that's also very easy to get away with."

Q "Drinking is allowed in dorm rooms, but drugs will get you kicked out of school. **There's a lot of drug use going on off-campus** though, and no one gets caught. Even if you're only 12, if you live in the dorms you are allowed to drink without any worries about being punished."

Q "**Don't get caught**. Enough said."

The College Prowler Take On...
Campus Strictness

Students agree that you can basically drink as much as you want around Notre Dame and have little to worry about from campus authorities; at worst, the consequences will be about as severe as a slap on the wrist. On the other end of the spectrum, however, the penalties for both drug use and sex on campus are expulsion. Most students didn't complain about the university's priorities, though they are noticeably different from many other schools.

The bottom line? Drink if you like, but don't use drugs or get caught fooling around. The lenient alcohol policy leaves plenty of room for students to have fun; however, there are hefty fines for overindulgence. Students are expected to be responsible, and there is supervision – if you can't keep things behind closed doors, you will get in trouble for it. Make sure you consider the consequences before you do anything on campus. Don't push things too far and you should be just fine.

The College Prowler™ Grade on

Campus Strictness: C-

A high Campus Strictness grade implies an overall lenient atmosphere; police and RAs are fairly tolerant, and the administration's rules are flexible.

Parking

The Lowdown On...
Parking

Approximate Parking Permit Cost
$50

Notre Dame Parking Service
parking@nd.edu
(574) 631-5053

Parking Fines:
The first ticket is a warning; afterwards, tickets average at around fifteen dollars each. However, the fine for parking on-campus without a decal is around fifty dollars.

Freshman Allowed to Park?
Only freshmen with a GPA of 2.0 or higher are allowed to have cars their second semester.

Parking Permits:
Student parking permits allow parking in both the D6 and D2 parking lots, as well as the JACC (Joyce Athletic and Convocation Center) parking lot. Athletes are given special parking permits that allow them to park on lots that are closer to campus.

Students Speak Out On...
Parking

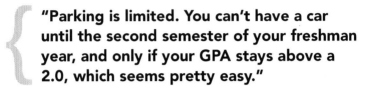

{ **"Parking is limited. You can't have a car until the second semester of your freshman year, and only if your GPA stays above a 2.0, which seems pretty easy."**

Q "Parking kind of sucks, and **you have to pay extra for the permit**."

Q "There is plenty of parking on-campus, but, depending on where you live, it may be far from your dorm. Keep in mind that when I say far, I don't mean a great distance, because **it only takes 15 minutes to walk from one side of campus to the other**."

Q "Sometimes you have to park farther away than you would like but **there are always spaces**. The lots aren't really near anything, but the campus is pretty much pedestrian anyway."

Q "Freshmen can't have cars until the second semester, but **the situation is pretty good**."

Q "There are two student parking lots, and **there are always spots**. Depending on where you live, you may have to walk a little farther, but it's not a big deal."

Q "There is always more than enough parking. **The only flaw is the distance from your dorm.**"

Q "**You may have to walk awhile to get to your dorm**, but there will always be a parking place somewhere. Football weekends, however, are a different story."

Q "Parking sucks. There aren't many places to park and **you can't get on-campus for anything** since they are so anal about it. So prepare yourself for a hike if you have a car."

The College Prowler Take On...
Parking

Finding a parking space on campus isn't that difficult, but you'll probably have a bit of a hike to get there from your dorm or classroom. All of the student-accessible lots are on the outskirts of campus – no one can bring cars into the main part of campus without a special permit from university police, and these only last for about an hour at a time. This can make it more difficult to haul groceries or move other things between car and dorm, but generally that's not a problem for students.

Unless you absolutely loathe walking to your car, you won't have to send your roommate outside with a lawn chair to save you a good spot. If you really are worried about it, however, you might do just that – some such incidents have been known to occur. Thankfully, though, the Notre Dame environment is such that most students hardly ever leave campus anyway. You won't have to trek to that far-off parking space often, and when you do it's never going to be much more than a ten minute walk

C+

The College Prowler™ Grade on
Parking: C+

A high grade in this section indicates that parking is both available and affordable, and that parking enforcement isn't overly severe.

Transportation

The Lowdown On...
Transportation

Ways to Get
Around Town
On Campus

Notre Dame/St. Mary's
Campus Shuttle, Monday-
Friday 7:00 a.m.-10:15 p.m.,
Friday evenings 10:20 p.m.-
2:15 a.m., Saturday evenings
9:00 p.m.-2:15 a.m.

United Limo Parking Lot
Shuttle, Monday-Friday 6:30
a.m.-8:30 a.m., 11:30 a.m.-1:30
p.m., 4:00 p.m.-6:00 p.m.

Transportation Services
115 Maintenance Center
Notre Dame, IN 46556
(574) 631-6467
undtrans@nd.edu

Public Transportation
South Bend Public
Transportation Corporation
901 East Northside Boulevard
P.O. Box 1437
South Bend, IN 46624(219)
232-9901
http://www.sbtranspo.com/

Taxi Cabs

ABC Cabs
(574) 233-4000

City Cab
(574) 233-2020

Exodus Cab
(574) 233-6000

Michiana Taxi
(574) 233-4040

Shamrock Cabs
(574) 243-5500

Universal Cabs
(574) 287-1313

University Cabs and Motors
(574) 288-7777

Yellow Cab
(574) 233-9333

Car Rentals

Affordable Auto Rental
(574) 277-8221
(574) 232-6332

Budget
(574) 287-2333

Dollar
(national) (800) 800-4000.
www.dollar.com

Enterprise
(national) (800) 736-8222
www.enterprise.com

Xxpert Rent-a-Car
(574) 258-5612

Best Ways to Get Around Town

Taxi Cabs
Shuttle
City buses

Ways to Get Out of Town

O'Hare International Airport
South Bend Regional Airport
Amtrak
Greyhound
American Trailways

Airport

South Bend Regional Airport
4477 Progress Dr.
(574) 282-4590

Airlines Serving South Bend (South Bend Regional Airport)

American Airlines
(800) 433-7300
www.americanairlines.com

Delta
(800) 221-1212
www.delta-air.com

Northwest
(800) 225-2525
www.nwa.com

Southwest
(800) 435-9792
www.southwest.com

Airlines (continued):
TWA
(800) 221-2000
www.twa.com

United
(800) 241-6522
www.united.com

US Airways
(800) 428-4322
www.usairways.com

How to Get to the Airport

South Bend Regional Airport is located about 5 miles, or a 20-30 minute drive, from the university. The easiest way to get there is to take Route 31 south of Notre Dame to the Lincoln Highway West. From there, make a right onto Maplewood Ave., a left onto Commerce Drive, and then another left onto Progress Drive. The airport will be right there.

A Cab Ride to the Airport Costs:

Depending on which cab company you call, a ride to the airport can span anywhere from five dollars a person (if you're sharing the cab) to twelve dollars for one person.

Greyhound

(574) 287-6041
(574) 231-2222
(574) 262-4406
(574) 935-3503

Amtrak

(574) 288-2212
(574) 684-1663

Travel Agents

Anthony Travel Agency, located in the basement of the La Fortune Student Center, offers reliable travel services. If you are flying out of Chicago and need to book a bus ride there, they'll book you a round trip for about $50. They also offer discount fares for visiting students and their parents; call (800) 7-Domers for this offer. For more information call: (800) 366-3772

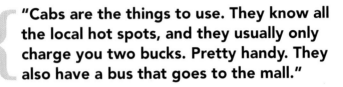

{ **"Cabs are the things to use. They know all the local hot spots, and they usually only charge you two bucks. Pretty handy. They also have a bus that goes to the mall."**

Q "There is a bus which is pretty cheap that you can take to the mall and some other places, but **it's usually easier to find someone with a car**. For the nightlife, there are $2 cab rides to almost every party location off-campus. So it's relatively cheap if you don't want to walk."

Q "**Cabs come by all the time**, and the South Bend airport is only 25 minutes away."

Q "There's **no real convenient public transportation**, but you won't really need it. The campus is fairly small, so you can walk anywhere."

Q "Public transportation is decent. **You won't need to get off-campus very much**. But my advice would be to take a car or make friends with people who own cars. It would keep you from waiting around for a bus or cab."

Q "**Taxis are usually the way to go**. Pack as many people as you can into one to save money!"

Q "**The bus is free with your ND student ID** and it goes to the bus station and to the mall... in other words, almost everywhere someone might need to go. It's kind of sketchy sometimes, though."

Q "The only place you'll probably want to go by bus is to the mall. There are a few bus stops on- campus, but the buses aren't always on-time and have been known to leave you stranded at the mall. **Use the bus as a last resort** or when you have a lot of time to spare, which will be never. Cabs are more reliable in terms of arriving on-time, but you might have a near-death experience on your ride to your destination."

Q "Public transportation is okay. **I'd still say it's better to have your own car**."

The College Prowler Take On...
Transportation

Although the phrase "public transportation" brings to mind bad images for many people, students agree that the cost helps you to overlook the conditions – buses are actually free with your Notre Dame ID. Unfortunately, the bus lines don't go all that many places that you're going to want to visit; use them to see the mall or to get out of town for awhile. The constant presence of taxi cabs on campus is a definite plus, especially on weekends; rides off campus are a mere two dollars, and you can get to some of the best party spots this way. It's best to split a cab with friends, not only because of the reduced rates but because it's easier to cope with the near-death experience of a taxi ride this way.

As far as availability and affordability, there's little to complain about with Notre Dame's public transit. Perhaps the greatest part of it, however, is that it is largely unneeded. The university's facilities make trips off-campus fairly rare occurrences, other than for visiting the occasional bar or party. With the availability of student parking, automobiles remain the rides of choice whenever you do have to leave campus. If you ever need to get somewhere, however, it's good to know that you have the option.

The College Prowler™ Grade on
Transportation: C

A high grade for Transportation indicates that campus buses, public buses, cabs, and rental cars are readily-available and affordable. Other determining factors include proximity to an airport and the necessity of transportation.

Weather

The Lowdown On...
Weather

Average Temperature
Fall: 52°F
Winter: 23°F
Spring: 48 °F
Summer: 73°F

Average Precipitation
Fall: 3.48"
Winter: 2.45"
Spring: 3.34"
Summer: 3.97"

Students Speak Out On...
Weather

> "Well, there can be good days and bad days. When it's sunny outside it's so nice – everyone is out on the quads playing Frisbee or laying out. We've had our crappy weather too, though, with lots of rain and snow. We really get all kinds of weather here."

Q "**Weather is great in the fall**; pretty much all the way until November it's sunny and beautiful. The winters last most of the second semester, though, and they're a gloomy mess."

Q "South Bend weather is crazy. **Fall is beautiful and normally warm**, but winter can be really harsh. It's not unusual to get one or two feet of snow and bitter winds."

Q "For about a quarter of the year, it's great, but the rest of the time **it sucks big time**. It could be worse, I guess, but the winters are tough."

Q "**The weather's crazy and unpredictable**. It can be eighty degrees one day and snowy the next. It usually starts snowing in November and doesn't stop until April."

Q "Honestly, the weather sucks. **It's probably the worst part of going to school here**."

Q "**Winter can last from October until May** – but I love snow, so it works for me."

Q "Weather is not one of Notre Dame's fortes. There is this thing called 'permacloud' that takes over the sky, and **you might not see the sun for a long time**."

Q "Bring warm clothes! **Notre Dame is ALWAYS cold!** We get maybe two warm weeks a year. Bring sweaters and jeans and snow gear."

Q "The weather in South Bend is nice and hot at the beginning of the Fall and Spring semester, cool and windy in September and October, and bitterly cold from Thanksgiving through Easter. **Have your summer clothes ready for the beginning and end of the school year**, but take plenty of sweaters, jackets and thermal underwear for those days when the wind chill is in the negative degrees. Head gear, gloves and scarves are also recommended for cold days."

Q "Ummm.....where to start? There's only one way to describe Notre Dame, COLD! **Here, the seasons are irrelevant**. Expect snow in October and even in April. However, you might just have a nice seventy degree day in January. Here, you learn to expect the unexpected."

Q "Okay, the weather sucks. It's Indiana – what can you expect? **It's gray, gloomy, and cold for about six months of the year**. I kid you not when I say people start wearing shorts when it hits fifty degrees. Even I wore shorts then! Bring warm clothes and get used to wearing layers. I hated it, but it's the only way to go. The good thing is that everyone looks like a snowman, so you don't feel bad."

Q "Fall and spring are nice, but winter can be brutal. If you aren't accustomed to cold winter weather and plenty of snow, **you may be in for a surprise**. You'll definitely need a warm winter jacket, a winter hat, gloves, and probably a good pair of boots for trudging to class."

Q "We have **soupy gray skies** most of the year."

Q "Midwest weather is very unpredictable. One day you'll be wearing shorts and the next day you'll be covered in snow gear. **Be prepared for anything**."

Q "Unless you're from Canada, **you will need lots of warm clothes** to survive the winter, and I do mean it when I say survive."

The College Prowler Take On...
Weather

No matter how familiar they might be with cold weather, most Notre Dame students spend the winters covered in down jackets so thick that they can't put their arms down, and hats and scarves pulled so tightly that all you can see are eyes peering out into the snow. One of the worst things about the seasons, however, is their unpredictability. There will be days when it's beautiful, sunny, and warm, right next to days when you have to walk around bundled up and shivering. At least the spring thaw gives you something to look forward to; until then, be ready with layers of clothing, a sturdy coat, and maybe even a sun lamp.

The College Prowler™ Grade on

Weather: D-

A high Weather grade designates that temperatures are mild and rarely reach extremes, that the campus tends to be sunny rather than rainy, and that weather is fairly consistent rather than unpredictable.

Report Card Summary

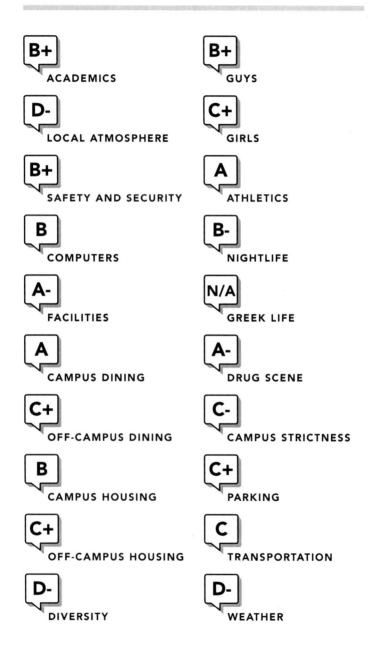

B+
ACADEMICS

B+
GUYS

D-
LOCAL ATMOSPHERE

C+
GIRLS

B+
SAFETY AND SECURITY

A
ATHLETICS

B
COMPUTERS

B-
NIGHTLIFE

A-
FACILITIES

N/A
GREEK LIFE

A
CAMPUS DINING

A-
DRUG SCENE

C+
OFF-CAMPUS DINING

C-
CAMPUS STRICTNESS

B
CAMPUS HOUSING

C+
PARKING

C+
OFF-CAMPUS HOUSING

C
TRANSPORTATION

D-
DIVERSITY

D-
WEATHER

Overall Experience

Students Speak Out On...
Overall Experience

{ **"Notre Dame is a special, special place, and I think just about anyone would find their own niche here."**

Q "**Despite the weather, I love it!** Everyone you meet at Notre Dame will leave a lasting impression on you for the rest of your life. The only way I'd go anywhere else would be if you moved Notre Dame to a warmer location."

Q "Overall, I loved Notre Dame. It had its ups and downs, but it was the best choice for me. The friends I made there and the education I gained were well worth everything. I'm glad I chose Notre Dame and I'm glad I learned so much from it. **I'm a better person because of where I went to college** and I hope that everyone feels this way when they graduate."

Q "I loved my four years at Notre Dame and **I think they prepared me exceptionally well** for life after college. Being a student at Notre Dame is an experience you can't find anywhere else."

Q "I personally loved every moment I spent at Notre Dame. I studied and worked hard, but I also partied a great deal and made many lasting friendships. **I don't think I could have asked for a more rewarding college experience**."

Q "I would recommend Notre Dame; it's a unique place that is basically unmatched. **If you want good academics and a great experience, go to Notre Dame**."

Q "I definitely love Notre Dame – it was always my dream to come here. I knew it would be some work. I have gotten involved in student government, made some great friends, and we have had more than our share of fun; but **don't expect Notre Dame to be like some state school with parties and beautiful girls everywhere**. If you know how to have fun, then you can at ND, but here, school should be your first priority. If not, then this isn't the place for you."

Q "School here was very hard for me, so I didn't enjoy it, but I don't know where else I would have wanted to go. **Notre Dame is a hard place to live – you're there to study and not have much fun, besides drinking**. Weigh carefully what you want from your college experience."

Q "The one problem I have with this school is that it's very conservative. **I wish it were a little more liberal** – for example, we have parietals (which is like a curfew for the opposite sex in our dorm). Stuff like that sometimes bugs me, but for the most part, it's not a big deal. I really enjoy the school, the atmosphere, and the 'family'. Plus, the academics and the athletics are very prestigious."

Q "In choosing Notre Dame, **I am absolutely positive I made the right decision**. I love it here. The classes are challenging, the teachers are outstanding, and the people are some of the most wonderful people you'll ever meet."

Q "I love Notre Dame. I have not once wished that I was somewhere else. You hear people talk about the Notre Dame 'family' and you think, 'yeah right.' At least, I know I did before I got here. **There really is a family feeling to the university**, though, and you'll believe it when you see it."

Q "Notre Dame really is a unique school. The people, the campus life, the education, and the atmosphere are all things that are really special to Notre Dame. Since I have attended a different school, I can tell you that **I appreciate the unity at Notre Dame** a lot more than most students. It really is like you are a part of a family. The amount of school spirit and love for Notre Dame is just amazing."

Q "I'm glad to be at Notre Dame – **the friends you make in the Notre Dame community are great and you meet lots of nice people**. The feeling you get the first time you step onto campus is indescribable."

Q "I considered it a blessing when I was accepted into the University of Notre Dame; and as a junior, I still think it's an amazing place where so much learning occurs both in and out of class. Notre Dame is definitely a top-notch collection of some of the smartest minds in the country. It's an intellectual paradise. **The university helps every one of its students succeed**; the only way you fail is if you try to fail. At Notre Dame I have learned so much about who I am, what I want out of life, and where I belong. Notre Dame is where I started to prepare myself for life, and I will always call it home."

Q "I had the most amazing time in the past four years and wouldn't have wanted to be anywhere else. Notre Dame is a special place and you realize that the moment you step on-campus. **Notre Dame has tradition and an amazing alumni network**. Come to Notre Dame!"

The College Prowler Take On...
Overall Experience

'Wonderful,' 'amazing,' 'special,' 'family' – these are the words that most students use to describe their time at Notre Dame. The university has a unique atmosphere that is embraced by many; the campus is basically self-contained, the dorms are all very close-knit, and there are truly strong connections between students. While the weather may test your survival skills and the administration may try your patience, overall the Notre Dame experience is unlike any other you'll ever have. The school's tradition and history create an environment where you'll feel welcomed the moment you set foot on campus.

Notre Dame is not an easy school, though, and it's important to remember that academics are huge. Above all else, you'll need to be willing to study and focus, or you're not going to make it through the university's workload. Students here are universally dedicated to their studies, and campus life reflects it. This is not a party school, and more liberally-minded students may find themselves frustrated by the value system or the lack of outside activities. The best recommendation for Notre Dame is to visit, and check out campus life firsthand; often, the atmosphere alone is enough to sway your feelings one way or the other.

The Inside Scoop

The Lowdown On...
The Inside Scoop

ND Slang

Know the slang, know the school. The following is a list of things you really need to know before coming to ND. The more of these words you know, the better off you'll be.

Arkies- a nickname given to Architecture majors.

Bun Run- refers to an event held during finals week each semester, in which the gentlemen of a certain dorm–usually Alumni Hall–streak the campus at midnight.

CoMo- a nickname for the Coleman-Morse center, which houses classrooms, the Campus Ministry Office, the University Writing Center, and the First Year of Studies Office. CoMo also has a study lounge that provides students with free popcorn and sodas as they study.

CORE- a class required for Arts and Letters majors during sophomore year that involves an intensive study of a particular subject.

DeBart- a nickname for DeBartolo Hall, the main building in which most students have the majority of their classes.

D-Hall- the abbreviation students give to both North and South Dining Hall.

Domer- a student at Notre Dame.

Domer Dollars- points that students can purchase from the ID Card Office that can be used to purchase food, groceries and bookstore merchandise.

Flipside- a nonalcoholic group that sponsors events on campus.

Frosh- a freshman at Notre Dame.

Flex 14- a student meal plan with 14 meals a week.

Flex Points- meal points allotted to students on the Flex 14 meal plan. These points can be used at other campus restaurants and at the campus mini-grocery store.

Frosh-O- the nickname for Freshman Orientation.

Golden Dome- refers to the Golden Dome that sits atop the University's Main Building. This term has evolved into a generalized reference to Notre Dame.

The Grotto- a memorial to Our Lady of Lourdes that acts as a place of reflection and prayer for many in the Notre Dame community.

The Huddle- the mini grocery store located in the La Fortune Student Center.

Kegs-n-Eggs- a traditional Irish breakfast of beer and eggs that takes place at Turtle Creek on Saturday mornings before home football games.

La Fun/La Funk- the nickname given to the La Fortune Student Center.

Mod Quad- directly behind North Quad, and next to the Hesburg Library, Mod Quad holds Siegfried Hall, Knott Hall, Pasquerilla East Hall and Pasquerilla West Hall.

Monk- nickname given to Father Edward Malloy, president of the university.

North Quad- located near North Dining Hall, North Quad houses Zahm Hall, Cavanaugh Hall, Farley Hall, Breen-Philip Halls, and Keenan-Stanford Hall.

O'Shag- a nickname for O'Shaughnessy Hall, which holds most of the Arts and Letters offices, a radio station, and Waddick's café.

Parietals- the hours during which members of the opposite sex are allowed to be in your dorm room.

Premium 21- a student meal plan with 21 meals per week.

Rally in the Alley- a party held at Turtle Creek apartments at both the beginning and end of the year.

The Rock- the term used to refer to the Rockne Memorial, a gymnasium named after Fighting Irish football coach Knute Rockne.

SUB -the abbreviation for the Student Union Board.

Super Senior-a fifth year senior.

SYR- stands for "Screw Your Roommate," a term that was once used to refer to the tradition of setting up your roommate with a terrible person for your hall dance.

Touchdown Jesus- the nickname for the mural of Jesus on the Hesburg Library, called "Touchdown Jesus" because it faces the Notre Dame Stadium and pictures Christ with upheld arms that look much like a field goal.

Quad- a term referring to an area of campus on which certain dorms are located.

• **God Quad**- located behind the Basilica, God Quad is home to Sorin Hall, St. Edward's Hall and Walsh Hall.

• **Pom Squad**- the female pep rally dance group; worshipped by Notre Dame men as 'the only hot girls on campus.'

• **South Quad**- situated near South Dining Hall, South Quad is home to Alumni Hall, Dillon Hall, Pangborn Hall, Badin Hall, Lyons Hall, Morissey Manor, Fisher Hall, and Howard Hall.

• **West Quad**- situated behind South Quad, Welsh Family Hall, Keogh Hall, O'Neil Hall and McGlinn Hall.

Things I Wish I Knew Before Coming to Notre Dame

• Yes, the weather really can get that cold.

• There are smaller academic programs offered, they just generalize them in the brochure.

• There isn't much to see in South Bend.

• "Parietals" – that word isn't in very many dictionaries!

• There are tutoring programs offered, as well as job and internship opportunities.

Tips to Succeed at Notre Dame

- Learn to focus and manage your time. There will be days when your work load will make you want to pull out your hair. Focus your time and energy into the classes that you feel are the most important.

- Learn to relax. It will be easy to get lost if you forget to take time for yourself.

- Don't procrastinate. There's a thin red line between relaxing and procrastination. The less time you waste, the more time you'll have for yourself.

- Don't take the professor's criticisms too personally. The majority of the professors are kind, but occasionally they will lend you a harsh word, be it on a paper or class discussion. Although this may be aggravating, it really does help you learn from your mistakes in the long run.

- Don't be intimidated by classes. The majority of Notre Dame students have never struggled with classes before. Once you begin to take classes here, you'll learn that there are some subjects that might not be your cup of tea. Don't let it bring you down.

- Get to know your dormmates. Not only will this help you become closer to those who live around you, it will give you a sense of dorm pride and enable you to meet more people.

- Talk to people. Speak up in class or start a conversation with someone in line at the dining hall. Despite the fact that many people may lend poor comments to students' looks, most Notre Dame students are friendly and interesting. You never know who you'll meet.

- Participate in intramural sports. IM sports are part of the Notre Dame athletic tradition. By participating, you'll not only grow closer to that tradition, but you'll grow closer to the people who keep that tradition alive.

- Go out and watch a game. If you don't feel comfortable playing sports, go and watch one. Whether it's varsity or IM, watching a game is great fun.

- Learn the football roster, the fight song and the Alma Mater. At Notre Dame, football is a religion, and, believe me, not knowing these things will haunt you at football games. Oh, and   remember – the only time Irishmen sit down during a football game is at halftime.

ND Urban Legends

Notre Dame is home to many student urban legends. Here is a brief sample of the most popular ones:

• The one thing that every Notre Dame student fears and avoids like the plague is stepping on the stairs of the Main Building prior to graduating. Legend has it that, if a student steps on the Main Building stairs before graduation, he or she will be forever cursed not to finish school.

• Guys, watch out: if a girl you are not really interested in asks you to take a walk with her by the lakes, take a trip to the Grotto, or tries to kiss you under the Arch in Lyons Hall, don't do it. Legend has it that the first person who walks with you around the lakes, goes to the Grotto with you, or kisses you under the Arch is the person you will marry. So unless you're in it for the long run, don't go.

• If you ever find yourself working alone one night in Washington Hall and you feel a chill run down your spine or hear a whisper in your ear, don't be alarmed – it's just the Gipper. The Gipper is Notre Dame's resident ghost. Once a field goal kicker, and, according to legend, somewhat of a party animal, the Gipp's school days were spent residing in Washington Hall. Back then, all students were subject to a curfew, and the penalties for breaking this curfew were much more severe than the slap on the wrist that students receive today. One night, after a roaring good time, the Gipper walked home in the rain and realized that he had forgotten his key to the front door of his dorm. Knowing that he would be seriously punished for breaking curfew, he spent the night in the rain on the steps of Washington Hall. Sadly, this night would lead to his death. The Gipper's time in the rain gave him pneumonia, and he died shortly thereafter. In the years that followed, Washington Hall was transformed into the performing arts center. Legend has it that drama students, working alone and late at night, have seen the old Gip' walking around laughing, making mischief on the stage sets, and scaring students out of their wits. Even though the sight of the Gip' may be somewhat scary, those who attest to seeing him say that he is merely a harmless, friendly, playful spirit whose legend is loved by all.

Traditions

Notre Dame is a university steeped in both history and tradition. A small sample of the everyday traditions includes:

- Standing for four hours during football games.
- Having your friends hold you in a push up position and throw you up in the air when the Fighting Irish score a touch down.
- "SYR" hall dances.
- Lighting a candle at the Grotto before exams. Whether Catholic or not, all students agree that a little divine intervention on test days is a plus.

Finding a Job or Internship

The Lowdown On...
Finding a Job or Internship

Most counselors will tell you that it is imperative to apply for and attain internships as soon as possible. Basically, you are expected to make yourself look good on paper. Most students begin to apply for internships the summer before their junior year. Now, around January of your sophomore year, all your friends will be freaking out, begging professors for letters of recommendation, and competing against each other for coveted positions. If, by chance, you don't get an internship right away, don't freak out. There are hundreds of opportunities; you just have to know where to look.

Advice

Start looking early. Notre Dame has a Career Center that is widely underused. If you prepare a preliminary resume and take it into the center, someone will sit with you and help you to spice it up, no matter how boring you might think it is. The Career Center also has the names of thousands of different companies and lists of careers that you can pursue with your major. You'll be surprised at the possibilities. Furthermore, there is an Internet service that allows Notre Dame students to post their resumes and look for jobs online. Finally, as simple as it sounds, read all of your e-mail! Both the Career Center and the different academic departments are always sending out mass e-mails detailing available scholarships and internships.

Career Center Resources & Services

Resume assistance

Internship searches

Career counseling

The Notre Dame Career Center

248 Flanner Hall

(574) 631-3355

http://careercenter.nd.edu/

ndcps@nd.edu

Graduates Who Enter The Job Market Within Six Months:

48%

Firms that Most Frequently Hire Graduates:

Deloitte & Touche

KPMG

Price Waterhouse Coopers

Notre Dame

Accenture

Ernst & Young

Alumni

The Lowdown On...
Alumni

Alumni President:
John Studebaker, Class of 1962

Email:
jstudebaker62@yahoo.com

Office:
100 Eck Center, Notre Dame, IN 46556
(574) 631-6000
alumweb@nd.edu

Famous Notre Dame Alums:
Regis Philbin
Joe Montana
Nicholas Sparks
Paul Hornung
Phil Donahue
Condoleeza Rice

Services Available

Notre Dame is famous for its extensive alumni network. Rumor has it that there is an alumni club in almost every city in the country. The Alumni Association helps to coordinate activities of 211 domestic clubs and 42 international chapters. Alumni club activities range from game parties to welcome-home bashes for students returning for the summer, and to farewell bashes for new Domers preparing to begin their first year. The Alumni Reunion Weekend is traditionally held during the first weekend in June. The greatest perk of the Notre Dame alumni network is that they look out for fellow Irishmen. From letters of recommendation to job placement, the Notre Dame alumni take good care of each other.

For more information concerning Notre Dame alumni and for the location of the closest alumni club near you, check out: http://alumni.nd.edu/

Student Organizations

This alphabetical club listing represents student clubs and organizations registered for the 2003-2004 academic year.

- Accounting Association, Notre Dame
- Adworks
- African Students Association
- AIDS Awareness/Students with AIDS Training
- Alpha Epsilon Delta
- American Cancer Society Club of Notre Dame
- American Chemical Society, Notre Dame Chapter of Student Affiliates
- American Civil Liberties Union, Notre Dame
- American Constitutional Law Society
- American Institute of Aeronautics and Astronautics, Notre Dame
- American Institute of Architecture Students - University of Notre Dame
- American Institute of Chemical Engineers
- American Society of Civil Engineers, Notre Dame Student Chapter
- American Society of Mechanical Engineers, University of Notre Dame Student Section
- Amnesty International Notre Dame
- Anime Club, ND

- Anthropology Club, Notre Dame
- Arnold Air Society
- Arts & Letters Student Advisory Council
- Arts Collective, Notre Dame
- Asian American Association of Notre Dame
- Asian International Society
- Asian Law Students Association
- Asian MBA Students Association
- Association of Art History Students
- Australia Club
- Bagpipe Band, University of Notre Dame
- Ballet Folklorico Azul Y Oro
- Ballroom Dance Club, ND/SMC
- Bands, Student Organization of the University of Notre Dame
- Baptist Collegiate Ministry
- Best Buddies
- Beta Alpha Psi
- Big Brothers/Big Sisters of Notre Dame/Saint Mary's
- Billiards Club
- Biology Club, Notre Dame
- Black Cultural Arts Council
- Black Law Students Association
- Bookstore Basketball Commission, University of Notre Dame
- Bowling Club, Notre Dame
- Boxing Club, Notre Dame Men's
- Boxing Club, Notre Dame Women's
- Brazil Club
- Business Law Forum
- Campus Alliance for Rape Elimination
- Campus Fellowship of the Holy Spirit
- Campus Girl Scouts, Notre Dame-Saint Mary's
- Caribbean Student Organization of the University of Notre Dame (CSOUND)
- Celebration Choir, University of Notre Dame
- Center for Homeless Children's Group, ND/SMC
- Chess Club, Notre Dame
- Children of Mary
- Chinese Friendship Association, Notre Dame
- Chinese Student Association
- Chorale, Notre Dame
- Christian Legal Society
- Circle K, Notre Dame
- Class of 2003 (Senior Class Council)
- Class of 2004 (Junior Class Council)
- Class of 2005 (Sophomore Class Council)
- Class of 2006 (Freshmen Class Council)

- Climbing Club, Notre Dame
- Club Coordination Council
- Coalition to Abolish the Death Penalty, Notre Dame Law School
- College Democrats, Notre Dame
- College Republicans, University of Notre Dame
- Community Alliance to Serve Hispanics
- Computer Applications Honor Society, University of Notre Dame
- Computer Club, Notre Dame
- Coro Primavera de Nuestra Senora, EL
- Council for Fun and Learn, The
- Cricket Club, Notre Dame
- Cycling Club, Notre Dame
- Debate Team
- Destination ImagiNation
- Detachment 225 Flyin' Irish
- Diversity Council
- Dome Designs
- Dome Yearbook
- Earthquake Engineering Research Institute
- East Timor Action Network@ND
- Economica
- EM3 - Minority Engineering Society
- Entrepreneur Club
- Environmental Law Society, Notre Dame
- Equestrian Club, ND/SMC
- Eta Kappa Nu
- Experiential Learning Council
- Farley Hall Players
- Federalist Society for Law and Public Policy Studies, Notre Dame Chapter
- Field Hockey Club, Notre Dame
- Figure Skating Club, Notre Dame
- Filipino American Student Organization of Notre Dame
- Finance Club of Notre Dame du Lac
- Financial Management Board First Aid Services Team, University of Notre Dame
- First Class Steppers of Notre Dame
- Flip Side
- Fly-Fishing Club, Notre Dame
- Flyin' Irish Color Guard/Drill Team, Notre Dame
- Folk Choir, Notre Dame
- Foodshare
- Forum on Biomedical Ethics, Notre Dame
- Gaelic Society
- German Club, Notre Dame
- Glee Club, University of Notre Dame

- Global Heath Initiative, Notre Dame
- Government Graduate Student Organization
- Graduate Student Union
- Graduate Theological Society
- Greens, ND
- Guam Club, Notre Dame
- Guitar Player's Association, University of Notre Dame
- Gymnastics Club, The Notre Dame-St. Mary's
- Habitat for Humanity, Notre Dame
- Hall Presidents Council
- Handbell Choir, The Notre Dame
- Harmonia
- Hawaii Club - Na Pua Kai 'Ewalu
- Health Occupations Students of America
- Helpful Undergraduate Students
- Hispanic Business Student Association of Notre Dame
- Hispanic Law Student Association
- Hugh O'Brian Youth Foundation Alumni Association, Notre Dame
- Humor Artists of the University of Notre Dame duLac
- Ice Hockey, Notre Dame Women's
- India Association of Notre Dame
- India's Development, Association for (Notre Dame)
- Institute of Electrical and Electronics Engineers
- Intellectual Property Law Society
- International Human Rights Society
- International Law Society
- International Student Organization
- Investment Club of Notre Dame du Lac
- Irish Dance Club, The
- Irish Fighting for St. Jude Kids
- Irish Gardens
- Irish Law Society
- Irish Marauder Drill Team
- Iron Sharpens Iron
- Italian Club
- Italian Law Students Association
- Japan Club
- Japanese Maritial Arts Institute
- Joint Engineering Council, Notre Dame
- Journal of Law, Ethics and Public Policy
- Journal of Legislation
- Judicial Council
- The Juggler
- Juggling Club, The Notre Dame
- Junior Parents Weekend

- Jus Vitae - Law School Right to Life
- Knights of Columbus, Notre Dame Council No. 1477
- Knights of the Immaculata, Notre Dame
- Korean Student Association
- La Alianza
- Lambda Alpha Honors Society in Anthropology
- Le Cercle Francais (French Club)
- League of Alternate Historians
- League of Black Business Students
- League of Black Graduates in Management
- Life Uncommon, A
- Lifewater, Notre Dame
- Linux Users Group, Notre Dame
- Liturgical Choir, Notre Dame
- Logan Recreation Club
- Lunch P.A.C.K.
- MadMacs Macintosh Users' Group
- Management Club
- Management Information Systems Club, Notre Dame
- Marketing Club, University of Notre Dame Undergraduate
- Married Law Students
- Martial Arts Institute, Notre Dame
- Massage and Relaxation Club
- Master of Science in Accountancy Association
- MBA Association
- MBA Business and Technology Club
- MBA Consulting Club
- MBA Entrepreneurship Club
- MBA Finance & Investments Club
- MBA Marketing Club
- MBA Women in Business Club
- The Medieval Club (The Worshipful Company of Our Lady of the Lake), The
- Memorial Hospital Medical Explorers
- Mexican American Engineers and Scientists/Society of Hispanic Professional Engineers
- Military Law Students Association
- Minority Pre-Medical Society
- Mock Trial Association
- Model United Nations Club, Notre Dame
- Ms. Wizard Day Program Team
- Mu Alpha Theta, Notre Dame
- Muslim Student Association
- Mystery Science Theatre 3000 Club

- National Association for the Advancement of Colored People, University of Notre Dame Chapter of the
- National Society of Black Engineers
- Native American Law Students Association of Notre Dame
- Native American Student Association of Notre Dame
- Navy ROTC Colorguard
- NDesign
- ND For Animals
- Neighborhood Study Help Program
- Net Impact Notre Dame
- Not-So-Royal Shakespeare Company
- Off Campus Council
- Omicron Delta Epsilon (Economics Honor Society)
- Operation Smile Student Organization
- Orthodox Christian Fellowship Club of Notre Dame
- Pakistan Association of Notre Dame
- Pasquerilla East Musical Company
- Pax Christi-U.S.A., Notre Dame Chapter of
- Pep Rally Committee, The Notre Dame
- Phi Alpha Delta Legal Fraternity, Hoynes Chapter
- Philosophy Club, Notre Dame

- Pi Sigma Alpha, Notre Dame
- Pi Tau Sigma
- Polish Club, Notre Dame
- Pom Pon Squad, University of Notre Dame
- Pre-Dental Society
- Pre-Law Society, Notre Dame
- Pre-Physical Therapy Club, N.D.
- Pre-Professional Society
- Pre-Vet Club of the University of Notre Dame
- Progressive Student Alliance
- Psi Chi (National Honor Society in Psychology)
- Psychology Club, Notre Dame
- Public Interest Law Foundation
- Ranger Challenge Team (AROTC)
- Right to Life, Notre Dame
- Rodeo Club, Notre Dame
- Rowing Club, Notre Dame
- Running Club (Men's)
- Running Club (Women's)
- Russian Club
- Sailing Club, Notre Dame/ Saint Mary's
- Saint Edward's Hall Players, The
- Saint Joseph's Chapin Street Health Center Volunteers

- Saint Thomas More Society
- Scholastic Magazine
- Science Business Club, ND
- Service Network, ND
- Shirt Project, The
- Ski Club/Team, Notre Dame
- Silver Wings, Benjamin D. Foulois Chapter
- Social Justice Forum
- Society of Automotive Engineers, Notre Dame
- Society of Hispanic MBAs
- Society of Physics Students, The University of Notre Dame Chapter of
- Society of Women Engineers, University of Notre Dame Chapter
- Sociology Club, Notre Dame
- Sorin Rifle Team - Army ROTC
- Spanish Club, University of Notre Dame
- Special Friends Club of Notre Dame
- Sports Business Club - MBA
- Squash Club, Notre Dame
- Student - Alumni Relations Group
- Student Bar Association
- Student Broadcasting of Notre Dame
- Student Business Board
- Student Government
- Student International Business Council
- Student Players, The Notre Dame Student Senate
- Student Union Board
- Students for Environmental Action
- Super Sibs
- Swing Club
- Tau Beta Pi
- Teamwork for Tomorrow of Notre Dame
- Texas Club, The
- Toastmasters International, Notre Dame
- Trident Naval Society
- Troop Notre Dame
- Ultimate Frisbee Club, Notre Dame
- University Young Life
- Vietnamese Student Association of Notre Dame
- Voices of Faith Gospel Choir, University of Notre Dame
- Volleyball, Men's Club Notre Dame
- Wabruda, The
- Water Polo Club, Men's
- Water Polo Club, Women's Notre Dame duLac
- Women's Legal Forum
- Women's Liturgical Choir
- Women's Resource Center
- World Hunger Coalition
- World Taekwondo Federation Club (WTF)
- WSND
- WVFI

The Best &
The Worst

The Ten **BEST** Things About ND:

1 The friends you make

2 The classroom experience

3 Irish football!

4 Awesome facilities

5 Dorm life

6 Road trips to away games

7 Bookstore sales

8 Shakes at the Huddle Mart

9 (For the guys) The Pom Squad

10 (For the ladies) The hot ND men

The Ten WORST Things About ND:

1 The weather

2 Parietals

3 The lack of diversity

4 CORE

5 All-nighters (of studying)

6 Spicy Sea Nuggets (probably the one bad thing served in the dining hall)

7 The smell of Ethanol floating through the campus (there is a chemical plant on the outskirts of campus)

8 Administrations policies (stringent alcohol policies, etc.)

9 Classes that occasionally get overwhelming

10 South Bend

Visiting Notre Dame

The Lowdown On...
Visiting Notre Dame

Hotel Information

For a complete list of Hotel accommodations in the Notre Dame area check out: http://aolsvc.digitalcity/southbend/

The Morris Inn

Notrte Dame Ave.
Notre Dame, IN
(574) 631-2000
Price Range: $110-$148

The Jamison Inn

1404 Ivy Rd.
South Bend, IN 46637
(574) 277-6500
Price Range: $70-$90

Signature Inn

215 S. Dixie Way
South Bend, IN 46637
(574) 277-3211
Price Range: from $68.57

➜

Holiday Inn University Area
515 N. Dixie Way
South Bend, IN 46637
(574) 272-6600
Price Range: $84-$130

Howard Johnson
146 S. Dixie Way
South Bend, IN 46637
(574) 272-7900
Price Range: from $44.33

Residence Inn by Marriott
716 N. Niles Ave.
South Bend, IN 46617
(574) 289-5555
Price Range: from $99

Queen Anne Bed and Breakfast Inn
420 W. Washington St.
South Bend, IN 46601
(574) 234-5959
Price Range: $65-$105

EconoLodge
3233 Lincoln Way
South Bend, IN 46628
(574) 232-9019
Price Range: $45-$79.95

Oliver Inn Bed and Breakfast
630 Washington St.
South Bend, IN 46601
(574) 232-4545
Price Range: $95-$265

Take a Campus Virtual Tour

http://admissions.nd.edu/virtualtour/

Campus Tours

To schedule a group information session or interview, call (574) 631-7505, or click on the link at the "Undergraduate Admissions" section of Notre Dame's website.

Information sessions are available in January/February on Saturdays only at 9:00 a.m. and 10:15 a.m.; in March/April, Monday-Friday at 10:00 a.m. and 2:00 p.m., and Saturday at 9:00 a.m. and 10:15 a.m. From May through August, sessions are Monday-Friday at 10 a.m. and 2:00 p.m.; and from September-December, Monday-Friday 10:00 a.m. and 2:00 p.m. and Saturdays at 9:00 a.m. and 10:15 a.m. During the football season, information sessions on home game Fridays are at 9:00 a.m., 10:00 a.m., 1:00 p.m., 2:00 p.m., and 3:15 p.m. Home football Saturday sessions are at 9:00 a.m. and 10:15 a.m.
Campus tours begin one hour after the starting time for the information interviews. There are no campus tours on home football Saturdays.

A word of caution: Notre Dame's website advises that, during home football weekends, finding accommodations and parking near campus is "nearly impossible."

The best way to know whether or not a school is the right place for you is to arrange a visit. If you are interested in visiting the campus for yourself, Notre Dame offers the Student Hospitality Program to high school seniors during the Fall Semester. This program provides overnight on-campus accommodations with current Notre Dame student hosts, allowing prospective students to get a feel for dorm life, attend classes with their host, etc.

For more information on this and other visitation programs, visit: http://admissions.nd.edu/cometovisit/

Directions to Campus

The University of Notre Dame is located south of Interstate 80/90 (Indiana toll road) and east of Indiana 933. Take exit 77 off the toll road and turn south onto Indiana 933. Turn east onto Angela Boulevard, drive for approximately one mile and turn north onto Notre Dame Avenue. Visitor parking costs $2

Words to Know

Academic Probation – A student can receive this if they fail to keep up with their school's academic minimums. Those who are unable to improve their grades after receiving this warning can possibly face dismissal.

Beer Pong / Beirut – A drinking game with numerous cups of beer arranged in a particular pattern on each side of a table. The goal is to get a ping pong ball into one of the opponent's cups by throwing the ball or hitting it with a paddle. If the ball lands in a cup, the opponent is required to drink the beer.

Bid – An invitation from a fraternity or sorority to pledge their specific house.

Blue-Light Phone – Brightly-colored phone posts with a blue light bulb on top. These phones exist for security purposes and are located at various outside locations around most campuses. If a student has an emergency or is feeling endangered, they can pick up one of these phones (free of charge) to connect with campus police or an escort service.

Campus Police – Policemen who are specifically assigned to a given institution. Campus police are not regular city officers; they are employed by the university in a full-time capacity.

Club Sports – A level of sports that falls somewhere between varsity and intramural. If a student is unable to commit to a varsity team but has a lot of passion for athletics, a club sport could be a better, less intense option. If a club sport still requires too much commitment, intramurals often involve no traveling and a lot less time.

Cocaine – An illegal drug. Also known as "coke" or "blow," cocaine often resembles a white crystalline or powdery substance. It is highly addictive and dangerous.

Common Application – An application that students can use to apply to multiple schools.

Course Registration – The time when a student selects what courses they would like for the upcoming quarter or semester. Prior to registration, it is best to have an idea of several back-up courses in case a particular class becomes full. If a course is full, a student can place themselves on the waitlist, although this still does not guarantee entry.

Division Athletics – Athletics range from Division I to Division III. Division IA is the most competitive, while Division III is considered to be the least competitive.

Dorm – Short for dormitory, a dorm is an on-campus housing facility. Dorms can provide a range of options from suite-style rooms to more communal options that include shared bathrooms. Most first-year students live in dorms. Some upperclassmen who wish to stay on campus also choose this option.

Early Action – A way to apply to a school and get an early acceptance response without a binding commitment. This is a system that is becoming less and less available.

Early Decision – An option that students should use only if they are positive that a place is their dream school. If a student applies to a school using the early decision option and is admitted, they are required and bound to attend that university. Admission rates are usually higher with early decision students because the school knows that a student is making them their first choice.

Ecstasy – An illegal drug. Also known as "E" or "X," ecstasy looks like a pill and most resembles an aspirin. Considered a party drug, ecstasy is very dangerous and can be deadly.

Ethernet – An extremely fast internet connection that is usually available in most university-owned residence halls. To use an Ethernet connection properly, a student will need a network card and cable for their computer.

Fake ID – A counterfeit identification card that contains false information. Most commonly, students get fake IDs and change their birthdates so that they appear to be older than 21 (of legal drinking age). Even though it is illegal, many college students have fake IDs in hopes of purchasing alcohol or getting into bars.

Frosh – Slang for "freshmen."

Hazing – Initiation rituals that must be completed for membership into some fraternities or sororities. Numerous universities have outlawed hazing due to its degrading or dangerous requirements.

Sports (IMs) – A popular, and usually free, student activity where students create teams and compete against other groups for fun. These sports vary in competitiveness and can include a range of activities—everything from billiards to water polo. IM sports are a great way to meet people with similar interests.

Keg – Officially called a half barrel, a keg contains roughly 200 12-ounce servings of beer and is often found at college parties.

LSD – An illegal drug. Also known as acid, this hallucinogenic drug most commonly resembles a tab of paper.

Marijuana – An illegal drug. Also known as weed or pot; besides alcohol, marijuana is one of the most commonly-found drugs on campuses across the country.

Major –The focal point of a student's college studies; a specific topic that is studied for a degree. Examples of majors include physics, English, history, computer science, economics, business, and music. Many students decide on a specific major before arriving on campus, while others are simply "undecided" and figure it out later. Those who are extremely interested in two areas can also choose to double major.

Meal Block – The equivalent of one meal. Students on a "meal plan" usually receive a fixed number of meals per week. Each meal, or "block," can be redeemed at the school's dining facilities in place of cash. More often than not, if a student fails to use their weekly allotment of meal blocks, they will be forfeited.

Minor – An additional focal point in a student's education. Often serving as a compliment or addition to a student's main area of focus, a minor has fewer requirements and prerequisites to fulfill than a major. Minors are not required for graduation from most schools; however some students who want to further explore many different interests choose to have both a major and a minor.

Mushrooms – An illegal drug. Also known as "shrooms," this drug looks like regular mushrooms but are extremely hallucinogenic.

Off-Campus Housing – Housing from a particular landlord or rental group that is not affiliated with the university. Depending on the college, off-campus housing can range from extremely popular to non-existent. Those students who choose to live off campus are typically given more freedom, but they also have to deal with things such as possible subletting scenarios, furniture, and bills. In addition to these factors, rental prices and distance often affect a student's decision to move off campus.

Office Hours – Time that teachers set aside for students who have questions about the coursework. Office hours are a good place for students to go over any problems and to show interest in the subject material.

Pledging – The time after a student has gone through rush, received a bid, and has chosen a particular fraternity or sorority they would like to join. Pledging usually lasts anywhere from one to two semesters. Once the pledging period is complete and a particular student has done everything that is required to become a member, they are considered a brother or sister. If a fraternity or a sorority would decide to "haze" a group of students, these initiation rituals would take place during the pledging period.

Private Institution – A school that does not use taxpayers dollars to help subsidize education costs. Private schools typically cost more than public schools and are usually smaller.

Prof – Slang for "professor."

Public Institution – A school that uses taxpayers dollars to help subsidize education costs. Public schools are often a good value for in-state residents and tend to be larger than most private colleges.

Quarter System (sometimes referred to as the Trimester System) – A type of academic calendar system. In this setup, students take classes for three academic periods. The first quarter usually starts in late September or early October and concludes right before Christmas. The second quarter usually starts around early to mid–January and finishes up around March or April. The last quarter, or "third quarter," usually starts in late March or early April and finishes up in late May or Mid-June. The fourth quarter is summer. The major difference between the quarter system and semester system is that students take more courses but with less coverage.

RA (Resident Assistant) – A student leader who is assigned to a particular floor in a dormitory in order to help to the other students who live there. A RA's duties include ensuring student safety and providing guidance or assistance wherever possible.

Recitation – An extension of a specific course; a "review" session of sorts. Because some classes are so large, recitations offer a setting with fewer students where students can ask questions and get help from professors or TAs in a more personalized environment. As a result, it is common for most large lecture classes to be supplemented with recitations.

Rolling Admissions – A form of admissions. Most commonly found at public institutions, schools with this type of policy continue to accept students throughout the year until their class sizes are met. For example, some schools begin accepting students as early as December and will continue to do so until April or May.

Room and Board – This is typically the combined cost of a university-owned room and a meal plan.

Room Draw/Housing Lottery – A common way to pick on-campus room assignments for the following year. If a student decides to remain in university-owned housing, they are assigned a unique number that, along with seniority, is used to choose their new rooms for the next year.

Rush – The period in which students can meet the brothers and sisters of a particular chapter and find out if a given fraternity or sorority is right for them. Rushing a fraternity or a sorority is not a requirement at any school. The goal of rush is to give students who are serious about pledging a feel for what to expect.

Semester System – The most common type of academic calendar system at college campuses. This setup typically includes two semesters in a given school year. The "fall" semester starts around the end of August or early September and finishes right before winter vacation. The "spring" semester usually starts in mid-January and ends around late April or May.

Student Center/Rec Center/Student Union – A common area on campus that often contains study areas, recreation facilities, and eateries. This building is often a good place to meet up with fellow students and is most commonly used as a hangout. Depending on the school, the student center can have a huge role or a non-existent role in campus life.

Student ID – A university-issued photo ID that serves as a student's key to many different functions within an institution. Some schools require students to show these cards in order to get into dorms, libraries, cafeterias, and other facilities. In addition to storing meal plan information, in some cases, a student ID can actually work as a debit card and allow students to purchase things from bookstores or local shops.

Suite – A type of dorm room. Unlike other places that have communal bathrooms that are shared by the entire floor, a suite has a private bathroom. Suite-style dorm rooms can house anywhere from two to ten students.

TA (Teacher's Assistant) – An undergraduate or grad student who helps in some manner with a specific course. In some cases, a TA will teach a class, assist a professor, grade assignments, or conduct office hours.

Undergraduate – A student who is in the process of studying for their Bachelor (college) degree.

ABOUT THE AUTHOR

Whenever I tell people that I'm studying to become a writer, their jaws drop and they give me a look of pity as though I were already a starving artist. Well, I don't know if I'm on my way to becoming a starving artist, but I do know that deciding to write is the best decision that I have ever made. I would like to sincerely thank everyone at College Prowler for giving me the opportunity to do what I love to do; it has meant the world to me. And I'd like to thank my parents, my little brother, Roli, my grandparents, all my extended family, my best friend Jeni, and last, but not least, Chuy for all their love and support.

I am currently a senior working towards an English and Graphic Design double major at the University of Notre Dame, and if my four years have taught me anything, it is that choosing a college is one of the most important decisions a person will ever make. I have felt nothing but satisfaction with my choice, and I hope that every student who pursues a higher education will feel the same way. I sincerely hope that you enjoyed reading this book and that it served as a helpful tool in your college search. If you ever have any questions or comments, please feel free to contact me at AnikkaAyala@collegeprowler.com

Anikka M. Ayala

Notes

....

....

....

....

....

....

....

....

....

....

....

....

....

Notes

Notes

....

....

....

....

....

....

....

....

....

....

....

....

....

Notes

....

....

....

....

....

....

....

....

....

....

....

....

....

....

Notes

....

....

....

....

....

....

....

....

....

....

....

....

....

Notes

....

....

....

....

....

....

....

....

....

....

....

....

....

....

Notes

Notes

Notes

....

....

....

....

....

....

....

....

....

....

....

....

....

Notes

....

....

....

....

....

....

....

....

....

....

....

....

....

Notes

....

....

....

....

....

....

....

....

....

....

....

....

....

....

Notes

Notes

....

....

....

....

....

....

....

....

....

....

....

....

....

Notes

Notes

Notes

Notes

....

....

....

....

....

....

....

....

....

....

....

....

....

Notes

....

....

....

....

....

....

....

....

....

....

....

....

....

....

Notes

....

....

....

....

....

....

....

....

....

....

....

....

Need More Help?

Do you have more questions about this school? Can't find a certain statistic? College Prowler is here to help. We are the best source of college information on the planet. We have a network of thousands of students who can get the latest information on any school to you ASAP. E-mail us at *info@collegeprowler.com* with your college-related questions. It's like having an older sibling show you the ropes!

Email Us Your College-Related Questions!

Check out **www.collegeprowler.com** for more details.
1.800.290.2682

Notes

Tell Us What Life Is Really Like At Your School!

Have you ever wanted to let people know what your school is really like? Now's your chance to help millions of high school students choose the right school.

Let your voice be heard and win cash and prizes!

Check out **www.collegeprowler.com** for more info!

Notes

Do You Have What It Takes To Get Admitted?

The College Prowler Road to College Counseling Program is here. An admissions officer will review your candidacy at the school of your choice and create a 12+ page personal admission plan. We rate your credentials with the same criteria used by school admissions committees. We assess your strengths and weaknesses and create a plan of action that makes a difference.

Check out **www.collegeprowler.com** or call 1.800.290.2682 for complete details.

Notes

....

....

....

....

....

....

....

....

....

....

....

....

....

Pros and Cons

Still can't figure out if this is the right school for you?
You've already read through this in-depth guide; why not
list the pros and cons? It will really help with narrowing down
your decision and determining whether or not
this school is right for you.

Pros	Cons

Notes

....

....

....

....

....

....

....

....

....

....

....

....

....

Notes

....

....

....

....

....

....

....

....

....

....

....

....

....

Notes

....

....

....

....

....

....

....

....

....

....

....

....

....

Notes

....

....

....

....

....

....

....

....

....

....

....

....

....

Notes

....

....

....

....

....

....

....

....

....

....

....

....

....

Write For Us!
Get Published! Voice Your Opinion.

Writing a College Prowler guidebook is both fun and rewarding; our open-ended format allows your own creativity free reign. Our writers have been featured in national newspapers and have seen their names in bookstores across the country. Now is your chance to break into the publishing industry with one of the country's fastest-growing publishers!

Apply now at **www.collegeprowler.com**

Contact *editor@collegeprowler.com* or
call 1.800.290.2682 for more details.

Notes

....

....

....

....

....

....

....

....

....

....

....

....

....

Notes

....

....

....

....

....

....

....

....

....

....

....

....

....

....

Notes

....

....

....

....

....

....

....

....

....

....

....

....

....